Children
of the
Thunderbird

Edward C. Meyers

Illustrated by Matthew Varey

D1715413

hancock

house

ISBN 0-88839-264-8
Copyright © 1994 Edward C. Meyers

Cataloging in Publication Data
Meyers, Edward C.
    Children of the thunderbird

    Includes bibliographical references.
    ISBN 0-88839-264-8

    1. Indians of North America—Northwest, Pacific—
Legends. 2. Legends—Northwest, Pacific. I. Title.
E78.N77M49 1994   398.2'089'970795   C94-910119-2

Edited/Production: Myron Shutty

Published simultaneously in Canada and the United States by

HANCOCK HOUSE PUBLISHERS LTD.
19313 Zero Avenue, Surrey, B.C. V4P 1M7
(604) 538-1114   Fax (604) 538-2262

HANCOCK HOUSE PUBLISHERS
1431 Harrison Avenue, Box 959, Blaine, WA 98231-0959
(206) 354-6953   Fax (604) 538-2262

Contents

To my mother whose encouragement and gentle persistence over many years convinced me this book was worthwhile.

Preface

I am indebted to many people for this collections of myths, fables, and legends of the West Coast tribes. All of them have since passed to the "Land of Mists" but that does not mean I cannot proffer to them the credit which they are due. Many of their names, unfortunately, I cannot recall as too much time has passed—in most cases over forty years. To those I cannot remember, I give credit if only indirectly.

For the stories from the Lummi and the Quinault I am indebted to the late Isaac Martin who ran a small fishing trawler along the Straits of Juan de Fuca. From Adam Suwish, a chief of the Albernis, I learned of the foolish Raven and the less than tolerant Crow. The legend of the Deer and the Wolf people was told to me by Sammy Cardinal who in the 1950s was trapping near Williams Lake. Sammy also told me why a beaver will go to any lengths to avoid meeting a porcupine.

The story of Coyote Rock I learned from Agnes Jack. She told me the story one hot summer afternoon as we sat on the porch of her little house near Penticton watching over-ripe apricots fall from her many unpruned trees. These old friends are now gone but their memories remain.

I particularly wish to mention a very gentle man I knew only as Mr. Williams. He was very old and lived alone in a little shack on the shore of Lake Skaha south of Penticton. I was a thirteen year old trying to catch fish using a little wooden boat when he rescued me from my frustrations. He showed me how to bait a hook with a brightly colored ribbon, where to locate the fish in the deeper water, and how to "work" the line to attract the wily Kokanee. When the fish were not biting, he told me the stories of how five wolves and two bears became the stars of the big dipper and how the Coyote God caused and stopped the great flood. To him, a very special thanks.

The tales of the West Coast tribes all carry a message or convey a part of the history of the people who lived on the West Coast long before the encroachment of European explorers. These people cared for and nourished their environment. They took nothing from the land they could not use. They deplored waste and saw themselves as part of nature, not above it. Many of their stories praise the animals who they believed had been on the earth before them and had been instrumental in creating the land.

They placed their faith in trust of the Great Spirit who was their protector. They obeyed the laws of nature knowing that if they failed to do so, Great Spirit would show his displeasure by sending the fearsome Thunderbird who made fierce storms. But they also knew that the Thunderbird had been given the task of keeping evil spirits at bay so that no matter how bad things became, good times would surely follow.

After years of injustice induced by a succession of federal, state, and provincial governments; well-meaning but totally misguided missionaries; and white traders whose greed surpassed all bounds, perhaps at last good times will once again appear. It is hoped that Thunderbird will once again come to protect his children.

E. C. MEYERS

1 Tales of the Thunderbird

There are many legends in which Thunderbird plays a part. Some are very short, comprising little more than a paragraph while some are lengthy narratives. All of them portray this mythical creature as ferocious, giant, angry, and possessing great powers. In most of the tribal stories he is assumed to be second only to the Great Spirit in power and importance, though some have him farther down the totem pole with Raven above. Usually, however, his effigy tops the poles. He is often shown with outspread wings as he gazes outward across the land.

Thunderbird, to most of the story tellers, was the messenger of the Great Spirit. He created storm clouds, thunder, and lightning. He was a very private creature, demanding to be left alone. Few dared invade his domain. To offend Thunderbird by encroaching on his territory, it was believed, was tempting the worst possible punishment. Certainly, his disposition was such that none but the truly foolish would ever seek him out for social contact.

Thunderbird went by a variety of names. The Kwakiutl people called him Hohoq. To the Nootka and the AHT Confederacy he was Kw-Uhnx-Wa. He was always portrayed in the brightest of colors, mostly white, red, and black with lesser splashes of blue and yellow.

The Kwakiutl and Cowichan tribes believed there were a vast number of these birds. They also believed many of the creatures had taken human form and had lived as families in the Indian manner in lodges along the northern tip of Vancouver Island. These human Thunderbirds caused no problems to others as long as they were left alone, but should they be disturbed or molested in any way, they would change into their spiritual forms and exact a dreadful vengeance upon their tormentors.

The Nootka people believed Thunderbird to be a single entity, a powerful god in his own right. He had little interest in humans and certainly had no wish to act like them. He made the storms and produced lightning while hurrying across the sky delivering the Great Spirit's messages.

That he was the creator of storms was also the belief of the Haida people. The Haida, however, appear not to have greatly feared him. Their god was Raven who had no fear of Thunderbird, and because Raven was their protector, the people of Haida-Gwai saw no need to be afraid either. Still, they never went out of their way to incur his anger.

All the tribes believed that Thunderbird caused the storms and bad weather when delivering messages to the lesser gods. As he flew his great wings beat the air with such force that all the clouds were drawn together by the suction. As anyone knows, when many clouds gather rain follows. The beating of Thunderbird's wings also caused a terrible noise and that was thunder. He lighted the sky ahead of him with flashes of bright light from his eyes. Those flashes, of course, were lightning. Each tribe has its own version of how this phenomena came about.

Why There is Thunder and Lightning
A Kwakiutl Version

In the earliest days, before there were storms, Hohoq the mighty Thunderbird sat alone in his cave atop the highest mountain in the land. Hohoq was hungry and he scanned the coastline looking for a fat whale which would serve as his supper. For a long time he sat very still, his gaze sweeping the ocean in his search.

Suddenly he spied, far out at sea and swimming slowly as if enjoying the warm sunshine, a huge whale. That whale, Hohoq decided, would do very nicely as his supper. With a mighty push of his powerful legs Hohoq left the opening of his cave and glided smoothly into the bright sky.

Hohoq flew quickly toward the whale and, when he was directly above his prey, drew his huge wings close to his body and plummeted like a rock toward the whale below. Hohoq's huge claws were fully extended, ready to grasp the whale, and lift him out of the water.

The whale, however, had seen Hohoq approaching and, the minute Hohoq began his dive, the whale submerged to a great depth. When he resurfaced a few minutes later he began to swim seaward as fast as he could.

Hohoq, meanwhile, had managed to pull out of his dive just before he hit the water and had returned to the sky, waiting for the whale's reappearance. When Hohoq saw the whale again he realized the whale's great speed was going to be difficult to overcome. He flapped his mighty wings as hard as he could. Soon he was once more over the whale, but before he could dive the whale disappeared beneath the surface. Hohoq flew higher and circled about in wide sweeps.

The immense energy caused by Hohoq's flapping wings, however, had caused the air to churn violently for miles around until eventually all the clouds were pulled away from the high mountains. The clouds darkened the sky so the sunlight could not shine through.

The whale, realizing the sudden darkness was to his advantage, swam faster and faster. He hoped Hohoq would lose sight of him in the darkness, but Hohoq beat his wings harder and managed to keep within seeing distance of the whale.

The great noise from Hohoq's wings had produced a dreadful noise, so dreadfully loud that it frightened the Cloud Spirit. So frightened did she become that she began to cry. Her tears fell to earth in a torrent. So profuse were her tears that they fell all along the coast. The noise from Hohoq's wings was so loud the noise could be heard from north to south. So dark did the day become that all the birds returned to their nests, and all the animals returned to their homes because they all thought that night had fallen.

Meanwhile, Hohoq had lost sight of the whale in the dark-

ness that now covered the land and the ocean. But he was determined to catch the whale so he flashed great bolts of light from his eyes. The flashes of light illuminated the skies for a few seconds but each time the light appeared the whale dived beneath the waves and managed to avoid Hohoq.

Soon the whale was far away and safe. Hohoq, however, was unwilling to admit that the whale had escaped. He stayed in the sky for four days and three nights, all the time beating the air with his huge wings and sending bolts of light through the blackened sky. Cloud Spirit could not overcome her fear so she continued to weep great tears upon the land and the sea all along the coast. The clouds continued to blot out the sunlight; and the birds and animals remained in their homes afraid to venture out into the darkness.

Finally, on the fourth day, Hohoq gave up his search. He caught a small seal because he was so hungry that he was no longer greedy. He flew back to his cave with the unfortunate seal.

Once Hohoq had stopped beating the air and sending out the light from his eyes everything became still once again. Cloud Spirit, no longer frightened, stopped crying and the clouds began to drift back to the mountains where they belonged. The birds and the animals emerged once again from their shelters. The world resumed its proper condition.

Hohoq, meanwhile, sat in his cave munching his seal meat. He began to realize that perhaps clouds and darkness could be used to his advantage. He realized he might easily have caught the whale had the whale not seen him as he approached. He decided at that moment to always hunt when he had the advantage. In future, he decided, he would cause heavy clouds to form and he would fly above them lighting his way with the light from his eyes. That way, he was sure, he could spot his prey long before it saw him.

Thereafter, Hohoq hunted only after causing a great storm to cover his approach. That is why the world has thunder and lightning.

Thunderbirds were never considered likeable creatures. They have, however, been credited with some good

11

deeds that have benefited mankind. These stories always make it perfectly clear that the benefit was only a by-product of some act of vengeance because Thunderbirds were in no way interested in humans. This lack of interest, however, was never thought as meaning the Greatest Thunderbird was opposed to humans. Had he not been charged by Great Spirit to protect the world's creatures? Indeed he had, and he carried out those duties with diligence.

That did not mean he had to like the humans—it just meant he had to tolerate them. There are stories that tell how a Thunderbird brought about the abolition of slavery as well as others which tell how he caused warring tribes to cease their fighting and make peace. Generally, however, he was not inclined to interfere with the progress of humans. One story of the slavery issue is of interest in that it shows how this creature would make changes without intending to.

There is no doubt that there was slavery among the coastal tribes. However, slavery to the Indians was a far cry from the type of slavery practiced by many other societies. There is no evidence that any of the tribes depended on slaves to any great degree, but kept them mainly to do the unpleasant tasks around the village.

Slaves were nearly always obtained through war. They were considered property which could be traded or sold. Sometimes they were used as gifts handed out in the potlatch ceremonies. On occasion a slave might even be given his freedom. There seems to have been few families who owned a large number of slaves. Slaves were generally communal property used by the village in general and no one in particular. They were never, for obvious reasons, allowed to venture far from the village.

Slaves were never allowed to marry into a tribe, but they could marry within their own class. The slaves kept their own children and some tribes did not consider the children to be slaves. On occasion a tribal family would adopt a child of a slave and raise the child as its own. These children were integrated into the tribe and held full membership.

A slave could expect nothing of personal gain. At best he would be treated with reasonable compassion and some humanity. His only reward could be the granting of freedom or an exchange to a less demanding master. Exactly when the practice of slavery ceased is a matter of conjecture. No one can say for certain when the last slave was taken, but as late as the mid-1950s there were a few individuals who claimed to have been born of slave parents. As these men and women were by then well on in years, they would have been born before the end of the nineteenth century. Most sources indicate that slavery came to an end before the turn of the century. However, in the far northern regions, there may have been slaves into the early twentieth century.

According to an elderly native I spoke to while visiting Nootka Bay in 1953 it was the Kwakiutl who first abandoned slavery. I had no reason then to doubt him and have seen nothing since which proves him wrong. The many works written on the subject have failed to come to any definite conclusions, so I will give him the benefit of what little doubt I have. I did think at the time (and still do) that it was odd for a member of the Nootka nation to give credit for such benevolence to a decidedly rival nation.

The old man told me a story that took place in Quatsino Sound, a long inlet on the far northwest coast of Vancouver Island. With its three misshapen arms it resembles a badly malformed letter Z. Today the town of Halberg is located near the sound's northern arm, the village of Quatsino lies midway on the north bank of its middle arm, and the town of Port Alice nestles in quiet solitude on the southern arm.

Quatsino Sound was home to otters, eagles, cougars, seals, and small deer which flourished in the adjacent forests. Salmon teemed in the water from June until late autumn. For centuries the area was known to Nootka hunters and whalers as well as to those of the Kwakiutl nation. Its isolation and its length discouraged all but the very hardy from venturing deeply into it so only small parties of hunters bothered to go there.

The isolation suited the small bands who did inhabit the sound for it meant they were generally left alone. Those who lived there kept to themselves, traded with their immediate neighbors, and lived mostly in peace.

The old man's story was of this place and was part of his family legend. As all legends of the West Coast either include a moral or are based on some fact or circumstance, his tale may well hold some explanation for the decline of slavery. The following is his story.

The Thunderbirds of Quatsino Sound
A Nootka Story

Not far into Quatsino Sound there lived for many years a family of five Thunderbirds. These supernatural beings had taken on human form many years before and had spent the years fishing and hunting. The five, father, mother, and three daughters, had lived as humans for such a long time those who knew about them had almost forgotten they were really Thunderbirds.

One day a raiding party of Kwakiutl warriors paddled into the sound. The party, consisting of many warriors, came in a large canoe. Because of the number of warriors and the way they were dressed and painted, and because they had with them many others who were quite obviously prisoners, the Indians who lived on the shoreline knew at once the warriors were looking for slaves. The people all fled into the deep woods where the hiding was good.

As it happened the warriors were paddling past the home of the Thunderbird family when one of them spied the daughters mending clothes near the lodge door. The leader was overjoyed at his good fortune. He saw the girls as likely prizes. He ordered the paddlers to head the canoe into shore. When the boat touched the ground he and two of his men leaped out of the canoe and strode toward the lodge.

14

As the warriors approached the girls called out to their father who was working nearby. He, accompanied by his wife, hurried around to the front of the lodge. He stopped when he saw the warriors and raised his hand to indicate he hoped they had come in peace.

"We require slaves for our village," the warrior chief said. "We think you will do very well."

"I have little desire to become a slave," replied the Thunderbird human.

"You have no choice in the matter," the warrior answered. "If you do not come willingly we will destroy your lodge, kill you, and take your women. If you come willingly we will spare them."

"You are right," agreed the Thunderbird human. "I have no choice and I will go with you. I ask only that my eldest daughter be allowed to accompany me."

"I am a generous man," the warrior said. "Is there any other request you might have?"

"Only one," the father replied. "I would ask that we may bring our robes of bright feathers to ward off the cold ocean wind. As you can see we are land people and not used to the chill of the sea breezes."

The warrior, pleased because the two slaves would be all he would need to complete his requirements, was happy to grant the request. He waited while the two went into the lodge.

When the father and his daughter returned they wore their robes of bright feathers. The father also carried a small bundle. He asked the warrior if he might bring the bundle with him as it contained some family artifacts. The warrior agreed without thinking too much about it. He was admiring the robes of bright feathers. The warrior had never before seen such robes. He decided he would take them for his own when the voyage ended.

When the daughter and her father were seated in the canoe the warrior chief gave the order to push off from shore. The canoe glided easily into the deep water. The paddlers swung the bow about and the canoe, filled with warriors and slaves, left the sound and made for the open sea.

For two days they paddled until at last the warrior chief called out to the slaves that their new home was just around the point ahead.

"Make yourselves ready," he called out, "for your new home is just around the point of trees ahead. Soon you will be put to work for your new masters."

As he spoke the daughter and her father stood up and turned to face the warrior chief. They looked very fierce in their robes of bright feathers. The warrior sat in silence uncertain of what to do.

"Take my hand, my daughter," spoke the father. "Hold tightly. With your free hand grasp my bundle tightly. Be sure not to let it drop."

As he spoke the two began to rise toward the sky. As they rose their shapes began to change. They were no longer humans. They had become fierce Thunderbirds, one very large, the other smaller.

The warriors, very frightened, began to paddle as rapidly as they could toward the village. The Thunderbirds circled high in the bright sky watching the frantic paddlers below. Then the large Thunderbird took the bundle from his daughter. He took a thunderbolt from within and hurled it at the fleeing canoe. The boat was split in two pieces and those within tumbled out into the water.

When the large Thunderbird took the bundle from his daughter she swooped down to just above the water's surface. She called out in a loud voice and five sea otters appeared. They swam over to the slaves who were trying to swim to safety, gathered them all together, and led them to safety on the far shore. The slaves began running into the forest.

After the otters had gathered the slaves, the daughter called out once more. Five dolphins appeared. They pushed the warriors out to sea where they all drowned.

The smaller Thunderbird then rejoined the large one. The two flew over the village and, as they did, they took thunderbolts from the bundle and hurled them into the village. The people below fled in terror as their houses and sheds erupted into flames. Soon the entire village had been reduced to ashes. Nothing remained.

The father Thunderbird and his daughter circled overhead surveying their handiwork for a time. Then they turned and flew away, back to Quatsino Sound, where they rejoined the mother and the two other daughters. They once more took human form and remained as a human family for many more years. They were never again visited by raiding parties and may still be living there in peace and quiet.

2 When the Sky God Lived Among the People
A Haida Version

The quiet of the new morning was broken only by the mewing of sea birds and the raucous cry of gulls gliding in lazy circles overhead. The cold, gray water of the Pacific Ocean lapped against the rocky beach. Offshore, a pod of killer whales cavorted playfully in games of their own making. A light drizzle began to fall adding to the chill of the new morning. A woman, a girl really, of perhaps fifteen summers trudged along the deserted beach. She carried a basket made of woven reeds. The drizzle felt cold on her bare arms and she shivered as she walked.

Every now and then she stopped to dig in the sand with a stone knife with a long blade. Then she would reach into the shallow cavity and pull out a clam. Or she would hesitate in her travel long enough to scoop up an inviting mussel from under its sheltering rock. These tiny prizes she placed with the others she had harvested which had already nearly filled her basket.

Gathering had been good. She had nearly enough clams and mussels for the family's evening meal. She would even have enough to present a gift to the aged woman who lived alone in her lodge at the edge of the village. The girl often shared with the old woman who no longer had husband or sons to help her. The small acts of kindness toward the aged one made the girl feel good. The daughter of a Haida chief, she knew, must set good examples for the people.

As her basket was now filled, the girl turned and began to retrace her steps. It was then she spied, half submerged in a shallow pool of a backwater, a large cockleshell. The ripples of the incoming tide washed over it in gentle waves. The girl wondered how she had missed it before and hurried toward it.

18

She had gone but a few steps, however, when she saw a large eagle perched atop a boulder near the shell. The eagle seemed larger and more menacing than any she had ever seen before. The girl stopped in fright as her thoughts turned to escape.

"Stop! Do not run," called a shrill voice. "Come! Approach me. You are in no danger."

Startled, for she had seen no one but the eagle, the girl stood still, too frightened to move.

"Hear my words, oh daughter of a great chief," the eagle called to her. "I am Greatest Eagle. I have come to tell you that you have been chosen for a special task."

The girl, realizing the eagle was indeed speaking to her but feeling he had no thought of harming her, slowly approached.

"In the cockleshell," said the eagle, "is a male child. He is Tsin, the Sky God. Tsin has decided to live among his people. He has chosen you to be his mother while he is on the earth. You and your husband will raise this child as your own. He will be your son as he grows to manhood.

"When Tsin comes of age," the eagle continued, "he will return to his kingdom in the sky. He will endow you and your husband with magical powers and you both will become supernatural people."

The girl remained silent for some time after the eagle had stopped speaking. She was frightened and the words the eagle had spoken upset her.

"I know that you are Greatest Eagle," the girl replied at last. "And I know that you are a supernatural creature. I will obey your command, but surely you know I am not yet married or betrothed."

Greatest Eagle, always impatient and so anxious to depart, shifted his weight from one foot to the other then stretched upward and spread his great wings. The girl shrank back in fear.

"All is ordained," Greatest Eagle said. "You will soon marry and your husband will raise Tsin as his own son. Your years together will be happy. The man who will be your husband is also of the Haida nation. He is a truly good man and builds the great hunting canoes which are in the highest demand."

"I know of whom you speak, Oh Greatest Eagle," the maiden

replied. "But how will all this come to pass? My father, the chief, must approve. And what if the warrior does not wish me for his wife?"

"It is ordained," Greatest Eagle replied. "Your future husband is being told at this very moment by Greatest Sea Otter of what will be. And your father was told in a vision as he slept. It will be as I say. It is ordained. Open the shell. Take the child to your father now. He will make all arrangements."

With that, Greatest Eagle spread his huge wings and lifted from his perch with graceful ease. As the eagle rose into the misty sky the girl watched in awe. As she watched, he banked slowly toward the north. She knew he was returning to the misty islands, the forbidden land, the land of supernatural creatures.

Then trembling with uncertainty and fear, the girl went to the cockleshell and pried it open. As Greatest Eagle had said, inside the shell was a beautiful boy baby. The frightened girl took up the child and hurried to her village. She did not doubt the words of Greatest Eagle nor did she have doubts of her future. She was only troubled because the eagle had not told her why the Sky God had chosen her. She wondered as she ran into the village if she would ever know. Tsin was only a name she had heard from the village shaman in the stories he told the village children. She wondered why a god would wish to live with humans. Why would a god need a mortal mother?

"Father, father," she called out as she hurried up the ramp leading to the lodge's main door. "Father, this morning as I was gathering clams, I was stopped by Great Eagle who—"

"Yes, my daughter," her father gently interrupted. "I am aware of what happened. Come. We must prepare to make our tiny guest comfortable in his earthly home."

As Greatest Eagle had prophesied, in a few days the young woman was spoken for by a builder of the great hunting canoes. This man, a great artisan, had mastered the craft of canoe building and was well known throughout the land as a master carpenter. The man was aware that he and the princess had been chosen to care for the baby because Greatest Sea Otter had delivered the message to him as he was testing one of his canoes.

Thus it was that Tsin, the Sky God, came to dwell among the

Haida people. But for many years only the chief, his daughter, and her husband were aware that Tsin was a god of great importance.

The carpenter took his young bride and the child to live in a beautiful lodge he had built on the outskirts of the village. In the Haida style it was built very long and spacious—nearly forty feet in width—with walls of planking. The longhouse was supported by pilings of stout tree trunks which kept it clear of the damp ground. Notched logs leaning against a front porch served as inclined ladders for easy access to the door. The front of the lodge was decorated with brightly painted carvings. These and a tall carved pole related the heroic stories and feats performed by the carpenter and his father and grandfather before him. Like all Haida lodges it was built to house a large number of people, but in this lodge only the family of three would live.

The little family were together for many happy years while the child grew to manhood. He was taught to hunt and fish by his father. From his grandfathers he learned to carve argillite and jade stones. His father taught him how to build lodges and strong canoes. The boy, a gifted and eager student, learned all things quickly and his work was ranked among the finest in the entire land. Fleet of foot, he could outrun the animals in the forest, and the nets he wove caught many fish.

His mother taught him the tribal laws and told him the stories her mother had told her. She taught him how to weave baskets from reeds and how to carve tiny ornaments from shells and small rocks. The boy learned to mold pottery from clay. It was not long before his artistry became the envy of all the fine craftsmen in the land. Before long all the people knew that this youth was indeed a special person.

As the youth became a man his magic grew stronger. He could always find the streams in which the trout gathered. He could always locate the waters in which the fattest salmon swam. The people began to depend on him to lead the way, to settle disputes, and to make the decisions which they themselves should have been making. He told his mother and father that it would be best for all if he returned to his place in the sky for he was growing alarmed that the people were becoming too dependent

21

on him. Some were even talking of making him a king. His earthly parents agreed that he must follow his own counsel in the matter, that he must make this important decision by himself.

So Tsin, during his thirtieth summer, left his home one sunny day to begin a lonely pilgrimage to the top of a high mountain near the northern tip of what is now called Graham Island. There he stayed alone for fifteen days after which he changed himself into a wren. He flew high into the sky but soon realized he could not be seen from the ground because his color blended with the gray clouds. Tsin returned to the mountain where he remained another fifteen days.

When the fifteen days had passed Tsin changed himself into a bluebird and once again he flew high into the sky. Again he realized he could not be seen from the ground because his color blended with the bright sky. He returned again to the mountain where he stayed another fifteen days.

When those days had passed he turned himself into a bright woodpecker. He flew high into the sky once again and was pleased that he could be easily seen from the ground by anyone who looked up. He returned to the mountain, changed back into human form, and made his way back to his village and his parents' lodge.

The next morning Tsin called his mother and father to a clearing in the woods near the village.

"Oh, my mother! Oh, my father!" Tsin said to them. "It is time for me to return to my place in the sky and resume my rightful role as Sky God. The people have come to know me as a god so it is now time to see if they have learned the lessons I have tried to teach them. With your help I have shown them the ways of the supernatural people. When I am needed, if they call out to me, I will appear to them in the sky as a woodpecker. This sign they will see and they will know I am with them always."

Then he embraced his mother and father for the last time. He changed himself into the woodpecker and flew quickly to a branch in a nearby tree. For a very long moment Tsin looked upon his parents as if reluctant to leave.

"Before I leave," Tsin said to them, "I will endow you both with great magical powers. You, my mother, will become a supernatural person and will control the winds. You will be known for all time as Fair Weather Woman."

He then gave her the great powers which would enable her to control the winds and the weather that he would send to the world. Tsin told her she must go to the farthest tip of the largest island. There she would watch the skies every morning and every evening for a sign from her son.

"I shall give you the sign by which you will control the weather and the winds," Tsin told her. "You will see me as a great woodpecker as I fly across the sky. When I appear, the sky will be my red color. If you see me in the morning, you will loosen your magic robes so the winds may blow. If you see me at night you will close your robes tightly so the winds will not escape. If I appear in the evening, the following day will be fair.

"If I appear in the morning, the day will become rainy or windy. The fishermen will know what the weather will be because they will see me and will know if they should venture out."

Tsin then addressed his father. "To you, my father, I will also give great magic. You will also become a supernatural person and shall be known as Master Carpenter. I will allow you to stay forever with your wife whom you love so dearly, and you will always be together except for the occasions when I will send you on journeys to perform great deeds on my behalf."

Then Tsin nodded a final farewell and flew away. When Tsin had been gone a few minutes Fair Weather Woman and Master Carpenter returned to their lodge where they gathered a few of their most precious belongings. Then, using their new magic, they turned themselves into puffins. Then they flew quickly to their new home. There they would reside forever.

3 Why One Should Never Say, I'll do it Tomorrow

A Haida Story

One day when Fine Weather Woman and Master Carpenter were walking hand in hand near their home, a woodpecker landed on a branch close to them. The two supernatural persons were pleased to see the bird for they knew it was Tsin come to visit. The three exchanged some pleasant talk as some time had passed since they had seen each other.

"Master Carpenter," said Tsin, after a few minutes, "I have a special mission for you. I ask that you journey to the most southerly tip of the small island. There you will search for and confront the spirit that is Southeast Wind. You must tell him he must stop acting in his boisterous ways. Southeast Wind has become uncontrollable. The fishermen cannot venture on the sea because that mischievous spirit is causing the waves to overturn their boats."

The next morning Master Carpenter bade good-bye to his wife and, with long powerful strokes of the paddle, moved his canoe rapidly through the water on his way to the island we now call Moresby Island. He searched all around the island but could not find the wind as it had ceased its wild actions for the moment. Master Carpenter then paddled to a small island just off the southern tip of the large Island. This island is now known as Kinghit Island. There he discovered Southeast Wind sleeping in a large patch of seaweed close to shore.

Master Carpenter silently moved his canoe very close to the sleeping spirit, reached over the side, and grasped the spirit by the hair. The wind, now very wide awake, began to struggle with a great ferocity, but Master Carpenter would not let go. The wind spirit struggled to free himself but could not break the tight grip on his long hair. Master Carpenter tried to pull the struggling wind into the canoe, but Southeast Wind was very powerful and managed to remain in the sea.

The two struggled for five days and four nights, but neither could best the other. Finally the wind spirit began to tire and he called out in a loud voice to his relatives requesting them to assist him in his struggle.

First to arrive was Wild Wind who sent forth a hurricane, but it could not force Master Carpenter to release his hold on Southeast Wind. Wild Wind soon gave up his efforts.

Then Waterspout Spirit arrived. He sucked up sand and gravel from the bottom of the sea which he rained down on Master Carpenter's head. He was also unable to force the supernatural person to let go of the wind spirit's hair. He, too, gave up his struggle.

Sea Mist arrived next. This spirit hoped to cause the supernatural person to lose his way on the ocean. His magic was not strong enough to prevail against that of Master Carpenter. Sea Mist also went away, defeated.

Finally, a particularly evil spirit called Tidal Wave came to help his cousin, the wind. Tidal Wave was very powerful and he managed to upset Master Carpenter's canoe. But even this did not force Master Carpenter to release his grip from Southeast Wind's hair. Tidal Wave washed the pair up onto the shore. There they lay, both totally exhausted. They remained side by side for many hours. Still, Master Carpenter kept his grip on the wind spirit.

"Enough! Enough!" the wind spirit finally cried out. "I cannot go on any longer. I have no strength left. You have defeated me in fair contest and I am bound to do your bidding."

"I, too, am exhausted," replied the supernatural person. "But I will not let you go until you promise to stop your boisterous ways. That is what Tsin has ordered me to do."

"I will do as you say," said Southeast Wind, "because you have vanquished me. Tell the Sky God I will stay within my season. In the future, I will only venture out during the winter months."

"That is good," declared Master Carpenter. "That is what Tsin commanded me to tell you to do."

"I will comply," promised the wind spirit. "I would not have been out at all had I not felt it necessary to avenge my mother."

Master Carpenter had never heard this before and he pressed the wind spirit to explain what he meant.

Southeast Wind then told Master Carpenter that the fishermen of a Haida village had been using his mother's name in vain ways. Master Carpenter understood now. He knew that the name of Southeast Wind's mother meant tomorrow in the Haida language. Her name was sacred and was not to be used improperly.

"How are they using your mother's sacred name unjustly, oh spirit?" Master Carpenter asked of him.

"Of late," explained the wind spirit, "the fishermen of the village are calling her name whenever they wish to defy their chief. When he tells them to prepare their canoes for the day's fishing, they call loudly that they are too busy to fish. They say to him, 'We will do it tomorrow.' By so doing they speak my mother's sacred name in the wrong way. I cannot tolerate such behavior."

Master Carpenter agreed that such behavior was intolerable. He promised to inform the Sky God all that Southeast Wind had told him. They parted company then and each went back to his own home.

When Master Carpenter reached his home, he called for Tsin who appeared to him. Tsin listened carefully to all Master Carpenter had to say.

Then Tsin left and sent Thunderbird to tell the people of the village that disrespectful mention of the wind spirit's mother was to stop immediately. The fierce Thunderbird delivered the message with his usual great roars. The villagers were very much afraid and promised to obey Tsin's orders.

"If you persist," the Thunderbird roared at them, "Southeast Wind will be given permission to venture out and cause as much mischief upon you as he wishes."

To this day many Haida fishermen believe that saying such things as "I'll do it tomorrow" will bring several days of the most dreadful weather.

4 Why Great Spirit Destroyed His Garden

A Salish Version

In the very early days, when the world was new, all of Great Spirit's creatures lived together in a spacious, beautiful garden in the land we now call British Columbia. In this garden lived the first man and the first woman. They were happy and enjoyed their lives to the fullest.

Great Spirit had made all things available to them. He had shown them how to build a house, how to make a sturdy canoe, and how to carve the totem poles which Man had placed near his house. The poles told the stories of the adventures which Man and Woman shared as the days passed. Man and Woman ate of the berries and the nuts which grew in profusion on the many trees and bushes in the magnificent garden. Their friends, the birds, gave them fresh eggs to eat. The streams and the nearby ocean gave them fish, mussels, clams, and oysters. They wanted for nothing.

The humans shared the garden with all the animals and all the birds, and there was only friendliness among them. There was neither fear nor distrust to disrupt life in Great Spirit's beautiful garden. All creatures spoke the same language and everyone helped each other in the daily work that had to be done, even though there was very little work to do.

Great Spirit had planned it so no one had to work very hard—just enough to gather the food that was needed or to make the repairs that were necessary should a house be damaged by some evil spirit which may have trespassed into the sacred garden. There were neither cares nor sorrow in the garden during the early years.

On warm summer days Man would meet with the animals and soon such meetings became customary. The group always began the meetings in the same manner as they discussed their latest adventures and told of their achievements. Their talks were always in praise of each other and songs of praise were sung relating the endeavor of those whom the group felt had made some special contribution to the community since the previous meeting. Great Spirit often attended the meetings in the shape of a small bird. He would perch on a branch and listen to his children as they sang songs of praise to each other. Great Spirit was very pleased with his children.

One day, however, Great Spirit began to wonder what his children spoke of at the meetings he did not attend. He wondered if they behaved the way they did because they knew he was present and were only trying to impress him. He decided to test them by staying away for some time then appearing in a disguise which none of his children would recognize.

Great Spirit stayed away from the meetings for many months. On the day he returned to the gathering he entered the garden as a tiny rabbit. He chose that disguise because rabbits rarely attract attention. He sat by himself in a far corner and listened intently. All his children had taken their places.

Everyone wanted to speak at once. They all vied for attention. With all the shouting there was much noise and a great deal of confusion. Great Spirit grew uneasy, but he said nothing and remained very still on the edge of the crowd.

Finally, Beaver outshouted everyone else and gained the upper hand. He suggested that each speak in turn so all might hear. The others agreed so Beaver, because it was his suggestion, was told to speak first. Great Spirit was pleased and thought to himself that Beaver was very wise because he had restored order. He soon changed his mind.

"I am great and my medicine is very strong," Beaver cried out in a loud voice. "I build dams and direct the courses of streams and rivers. I cause lakes to be formed. No one here does that."

Bear was not to be outdone. He rose to his full height and thumped his chest. "I," cried Bear, "am greater because I am

28

powerful. No one can defeat me in contests of wrestling and feats of strength."

But Cougar quickly leapt to his feet. "I am greater than all others," he roared. "My medicine is strong for I can run swiftly and silently through the forest."

The arguments and the boasting went on for a long time. As Great Spirit listened he grew angrier by the minute. Each animal eventually rose, each speaking loudly of how great a creature he was. Each in turn sang a song of self-praise as he told of his prowess and abilities. Great Spirit was just about to reveal his presence when Man stood up and strode to the center of the gathering.

"I," cried Man, "am greater than all of you combined. I am blessed over all of you. Great Spirit has given to me the ability to build houses, to make canoes, to carve totem poles, and to carve pictures in boards to glorify my house. I, too, can wrestle. I can run swiftly. I was given powerful magic. I am superior to all of you."

On hearing this, Great Spirit could no longer hide his anger. Still disguised as the rabbit he hopped into the center of the clearing and called out to those assembled.

"I am greater than all of you. All of you together can never match the magic which is mine. My magic surpasses all of yours."

The entire crowd laughed loudly when the rabbit finished speaking. They had no idea who he really was.

"Do not laugh," warned the rabbit. "I am about to show you my magic."

Then Great Spirit called out magic words in a very loud voice, so loud that the animals and Man cowered in awe. None of them had ever heard such a voice, and they knew this was no ordinary rabbit. As the magic words sounded the sky darkened and a great thunderclap was heard. The creatures all looked up in awe and were very afraid. Then a huge Thunderbird appeared in the center of the clearing. The entire group fell back in fright for the Thunderbird was the one thing feared by all of Great Spirit's children.

The Thunderbird stomped about in the clearing letting out loud roars. Everyone cringed in terror before the fearsome creature.

"I," roared Thunderbird, "am great. My magic is greater than all of yours could be if it was all mixed together." With that he fired a bolt of lightening from his eyes. The bolt split a huge rock into two pieces.

"Who among you can repair the rock?" he asked. "Is there anyone here who can match such a feat?"

The Thunderbird sprinkled dust on the two pieces of rock and they were magically fused together. Then the Thunderbird very gently picked up the tiny rabbit in one of his huge claws and placed it on the boulder.

"I," spoke the Thunderbird," am the messenger of Great Spirit as you all well know. The words I speak are his words. All of you here are equal in Great Spirit's eyes. All of you share the same space in his heart for he created you to serve him for all time. He gave you this garden so you could live together in peace forever.

"Now you have all grown vain. You have become arrogant. You have adorned yourselves with false graces. These things you have not earned. Neither do you deserve them.

"Bear, you are truly strong, and no one can defeat you at wrestling, but can you soar high in the sky like your cousin, the Eagle?

"Beaver, you can build dams to control the waters and cause rivers to flow in different directions. You can cause lakes to form. Can you also sing as sweet a song as your cousin, the Thrush?

"Cougar, you can run swiftly and silently through the forest. Can you also swim far out into the depths of the great salt ocean as does your cousin, the Whale?

"Whale, you can swim many miles out to sea and visit the farthest reaches of the ocean, but are you able to carve my likeness from a tall tree so to do me honor?

"All of you are limited to the talents which the Great Spirit has given you. You can do no more than that."

The Thunderbird then fell silent for a moment. He walked over to where Man was cowering. He looked down upon him for a long moment.

"Hear me, oh Man," said the Thunderbird. "You are the one that brings Great Spirit the most disappointment. You can do many things the others cannot and will never be able to do. The talents Great Spirit gave to you were given to offset your smaller size and physical weakness. Can you swim like Salmon or Whale? Are you able to sing as does Thrush? Do you run with the swiftness and the silence of Cougar? Can you win at wrestling with Bear?

"Children of the forest and the waters, you were all blessed in certain ways. There are differences, and that is how it was planned by Great Spirit. He placed you in this beautiful garden so that you could all play a part in his great plan. You were all intended to do the things he had planned in order that his world would always be a place of ease and peaceful existence. Your vanity and songs of self-praise have betrayed Great Spirit's trust in his creations. You have grown vain and have come to believe you are more important than you really are."

Then Thunderbird turned to face the tiny rabbit who still sat on the boulder. The fearsome creature once again took the tiny animal and held it gently. He held it out for all to see.

"There is but one who possesses the greatest magic of all, and that single being is Great Spirit." He then replaced the rabbit on the boulder and stepped back so all around could see.

At that moment the tiny rabbit changed into a glowing ball of light from which came a voice as thunderous as that of the winter storms.

"It is I who am all-powerful," spoke the glowing ball of light. "It is my magic which is the strongest magic of all."

As the voice spoke the sky began to darken and the sun was hidden by black clouds which had gathered.

"I created the sun to warm you," the voice continued. "I created the rain to cool you." At that moment a cold rain began to fall. "I gave you light to let you see and I gave you the night so you could sleep. These things none of you could have done. All

of you working together for thousands of years could not have done these things.

"You have repaid me with vanity and songs of self-praise. You have taken to quarreling among yourselves. You spend your time bragging of the powers that were given to you instead of using those powers for the purposes they were intended.

"From this day forward you will each go your separate ways. Each of you will travel your solitary trails, and, when your paths occasionally cross, you will feel for each other only fear and mistrust. Never again will you be able to sit together in council; nor will you ever again be able to call each other brother.

"This garden will no longer be home for any of you. You each will have to search out your food, and your food will be each other. Sometimes you will know hunger and thirst. Sometimes you will know sorrow and grief.

"But for all that, I will not forsake my children. I will still watch over you. If you call upon me in times of your greatest troubles, I will answer your songs of prayer. Sometimes, however, my answer to your prayers shall be *no*."

Then the glowing ball rose into the sky and quickly disappeared.

At the moment the glowing ball began its rise, the Thunderbird roared out in a terrible voice and the world was plunged into the darkness of night.

When the light came once more the beautiful garden was empty. There was no one left in Great Spirit's garden for, while the darkness had been on the land, the Thunderbird had removed each of the animals. He had taken them all to different parts of the greater forest and had placed them here and there among the hills and valleys.

But, though Thunderbird had taken the animals to places far away from the garden, he had placed Man and Woman just outside the borders of the garden. He had done this so they would not quickly forget the place which had once been their home. They tried to return but the mighty Thunderbird barred the path and turned Man and Woman away. After awhile they stopped trying to go back inside and the two humans began their new lives in a different part of the great forest far from the garden.

As time passed they forgot where it had been, but they never forgot there had once been a place where happiness was assured and where life was truly wonderful.

Man and Woman resolved that their children should know the reasons why life was sometimes so difficult. They told their children the story of Great Spirit's garden and then they told their grandchildren who in turn told their children. Thus did the story pass down through the generations.

This story was related to me by an elderly man who was a member of the Salish nation. He had heard it as a child from his mother. There is no doubt that it predates the arrival of white men as it is also told, with variations, by storytellers of many bands far removed from any Salish contact. Its similarity to the biblical myth of Adam and Eve is striking. Many of the tribal legends, such as those concerning the great flood, can find counterparts in the stories of many societies far distant from each other in both time and geography. The biblical myth of the Tower of Babel and the Makah tribal legend on the same subject are almost identical. They are probably both of equal age, yet the authors were separated by thousands of miles.

5 Why Blue Jay
is Held in Contempt

It is easy to feel sorry for the raucous Blue Jay because none
of the stories from the Pacific tribes show him in a good
light. This is unusual when one considers the vast differences in culture, location, and basis on which Blue Jay's
legends are founded.

For instance, one of the most important deities of the
Pacific legends is Raven. Raven was considered a most
powerful god by the Haida, the Tsimshian to the north, and
the Lummi of Puget Sound.

Raven, however, was no god to those who lived on
Vancouver Island. To the Cowichan and the Kwakiutl,
Raven was a silly bird, a moocher and a sneak-thief. While
he has a place on many totem poles carved by Island artisans, he is not given a place of high honor, certainly none
that compares with Thunderbird or Whale.

But, where Raven is either important or unimportant,
depending on the tribe involved, Blue Jay had no status of
respect among any of the tribes—anywhere. Poor Blue Jay
is universally pictured as a raucous, screeching pest. Sur-
prisingly, for all his frailties of character, he has more stories to his memory than any other creature—including
Thunderbird.

Almost always in disgrace, and rarely in Great Spirit's
good books, more often than not he dies for his foolish acts.
Despite his numerous deaths, Blue Jay always manages to
return to life, attesting his supernatural status.

Blue Jay, however, is not an evil creature and none of
his misadventures indicate the storytellers consider him to

35

be inherently evil. Blue Jay represents the human frailties of vanity, greed, and conceit—considered by the Pacific Indians to be the worst traits any human could have. A vain, arrogant person would be compared to Blue Jay and shunned by his fellows until he mended his ways.

To the tribes who inhabited the area we now call Knight's Inlet, midway along British Columbia's mainland, Blue Jay began his tenure on earth as a noble creature. Soon, however, he grew vain and became stingy and hateful. He is the original stingy person.

Blue Jay, it is said, caused a winter of great hardship which befell a large tribe many centuries ago. Because of Blue Jay's stinginess his entire village suffered the greatest of hardships. The villagers were ignored and shunned by others who would have helped had it not been for Blue Jay's refusal to consider their offers.

In time, Great Spirit was no longer able to watch indifferently as his children suffered. He sent forth his magic and removed the women and children from the village along with all the village slaves. Blue Jay, in disgrace, was then exiled from his people who turned to Raven for leadership.

The story is one of the best from that area. It was likely told to explain some terrible disaster that befell a particular village. The sudden disappearance of a major part of any village's population would need some explanation.

The way the story ends indicates Great Spirit fully intended to set matters right sometime in the future. Otherwise, Raven would not have been singled out to become chief of a village of warriors without women or children.

Had Great Spirit intended the village men to suffer permanent punishment for their foolish obedience of Blue Jay's wishes, he would not have allowed them to stay together. Neither would they be allowed to have the Raven's wise counsel. Great Spirit would have scattered them far and wide as exiles, or changed them into loathsome beings in punishment for accepting the vain and stingy Blue Jay as their leader.

Indian legends are generally quite explicit in their detailing of punishments that are meted out to erring creatures. By exiling Blue Jay and forcing him to become a transient bird, Great Spirit showed he was not about to tolerate infringement of his laws for proper behavior. On the other hand, he clearly demonstrated tolerance toward those willing to show remorse for their transgressions. Obviously Great Spirit felt the lessons learned by Blue Jay's followers would be lasting enough to keep them on the righteous path.

The Haida saw Blue Jay as a creature best avoided because he had incurred Tsin's great wrath and was rightly punished for his sins of vanity and boastfulness. Blue Jay does not adorn Haida lodge poles. He is not prominent in their carvings. He is pictured in their stories as nothing more than a foolish, vain, and boastful buffoon who never wins.

The inland tribes—the Salish, Chinook, Nicola, and others—considered Blue Jay to be a thief and a poltroon, a sorry creature with no redeeming virtues. Blue Jay was the epitome of braggadocio and vanity. The Pacific natives were tolerant of frailties but vanity and bragging were frowned on. Indeed, they were allowed only during the dances and ceremonies performed during potlatch celebrations.

Blue Jay was usually the one who took improper advantage of the free will Great Spirit had given his children. Still, it seems unusual that all the tribes, even those most isolated, depicted Blue Jay in the same light. It is almost as if his status had been discussed beforehand around the fires of a great council.

Why Blue Jay was Exiled
A Haida Version

Once, thousands of summers ago, Blue Jay could sing beautiful songs. So pleasing was his voice that he became a personal favorite of Tsin, the Sky God. Tsin told the people to pay honor to Blue Jay and to enjoy the beautiful songs he sang. The people did as Tsin commanded and were pleased to hear Blue Jay sing whenever he would condescend to do so—which was often.

Many summers went by. Each year Tsin gave Blue Jay another beautiful song to sing. The people listened to his melodies and delighted in them. Blue Jay liked to sing for the people and was never reluctant to sing.

Unfortunately, Blue Jay grew vain. He began to brag loudly to everyone that Tsin held him in the highest regard. He began to tease his cousins Thrush and Whitewing because his singing was better than theirs. He lost no opportunity to remind them of his special relationship to the Sky God. Thrush and Whitewing grew tired of listening to Blue Jay and went to great lengths to avoid him.

So Blue Jay began to boast of his talents in the villages of the Haida people. They also grew tired of his bragging and began to avoid him.

Then one day Tsin overheard Blue Jay bragging of his talents to Sea Otter. Otter calmly floated on his back eating a clam, obviously not listening, but Blue Jay continued his bragging anyway. Tsin, in his woodpecker disguise, alighted on a nearby rock and listened as Blue Jay told the otter of his greatness. As Tsin listened he became distressed. Tsin finally called out to Blue Jay that he wished to speak with him.

Blue Jay, when he saw the woodpecker, thought Tsin had come to give him another song and hurried over to the rock. He began to sing for Tsin, but the god commanded him to remain silent.

Instead of praising Blue Jay, as the vain one had expected, Tsin began scolding him. He told Blue Jay to change his boastful manners.

"Blue Jay," Tsin told him, "you are but one of my many children and are of no more importance than the humble butterfly or sand crab. All my children hold equal places in my heart. It distresses me that you have come to think you are more important than the others."

Blue Jay was shattered for Tsin had never berated him before. He fell before the god and promised to change his ways.

Tsin told Blue Jay that he would hold him to that promise, then left.

Blue Jay did behave himself for awhile, but as time passed he fell back into his old ways when his vanity got the better of him. Very soon he had fully returned to his old ways much to the annoyance of all concerned.

Tsin, of course, had been watching the progress of Blue Jay's reformation and did not like what he was seeing. He sent a messenger to earth to inform Blue Jay, Thrush, and Whitewing that Tsin wished to have audience with them in a clearing in the great forest. They were all to be there, the messenger told them, at an appointed time three days hence.

At the exact hour of the third day the three birds were in the clearing awaiting the arrival of the Sky God. Suddenly the god arrived. As usual Tsin had chosen to take the form of a woodpecker. He stood before the three resplendent in his bright colors of red, black, and white.

"I have called you three into my presence because I have become very distressed to learn that Blue Jay continues to behave in vain and boastful ways," Tsin began. "I have watched closely and have decided I must take action. Everyone is complaining. Blue Jay has become tiresome to my children.

"I have also noticed that only Thrush and Whitewing have not complained. Such patience shall be rewarded."

Then Tsin, after sprinkling magic dust on them, flew away without another word leaving three very confused birds alone in the clearing.

Blue Jay was the first to speak. "I wonder what Tsin meant by that—" Blue Jay began, but he stopped suddenly for his beautiful voice was nothing more than harsh croaking. He tried to sing a song but the sound he produced was rasping and strident, a hoarse shriek that was not at all beautiful. He turned away in surprise and anguish. He was beginning to realize what had happened.

Whitewing and Thrush also wondered what Tsin had done, and on hearing Blue Jay's pitiful shrieking they knew that the Sky God had punished Blue Jay. They were still, however, confused as to how they fit into Tsin's plan.

Thrush then sang a song followed by Whitewing. It was then they both realized the magic Tsin had brought to them. The songs they sang were more beautiful than any either had ever known, and their voices were more melodious than ever. The Sky God had taken Blue Jay's talents and had given them equally to the other two. That is why these two birds have such fine songs and melodious voices and Blue Jay cannot sing a single note.

Blue Jay, deeply humiliated, slunk off alone into the forest. He snuck into his lodge under cover of darkness and refused to speak to anyone for several days. He even tried to hide from N'mishik, his wife, but that proved impossible so he eventually told her what had happened in the forest clearing.

N'mishik, a squirrel, was none too bright herself. She tried first to console her husband, then she suggested that Tsin might relent after a few days. After several weeks passed, both realized such a hope was forlorn.

N'mishik then suggested to Blue Jay that he travel to the misty lands where the supernatural people live. She suggested he seek them out and beg them to intercede for him with Tsin. N'mishik felt the supernatural people might be able to work enough magic over him to at least restore his pleasant voice.

Blue Jay thought the idea worth the effort so he loaded his canoe with enough food for several days and paddled north toward the misty islands. By the time he arrived, however, he had forgotten that vanity had been the very cause of his disgrace. He was no sooner ashore in the land of the supernatural people than he began to brag to the first ones he met, a group of three shadowy figures. He greeted them by informing them who he was and that Tsin had given him great talents and had always considered him to be the best singer of all the birds. Blue Jay could not help boasting even when he knew he should remain humble.

The three supernatural people knew who he was. They knew all about him and his fall from grace. However, they let him prattle on.

"We have heard of you, of course, Blue Jay," one of the ghostly trio said at last. "Indeed, we know all about you and your great talents."

"In that case," cried Blue Jay, "you are well aware of my qualities. You know I am a great singer. You know I am a great canoeist and a mighty fisherman and hunter. Yet, for all my exploits I am nothing if I am unable to sing as I once did. I implore you to restore my wonderful voice. I will sing songs of praise and so do you great honor."

The supernatural people knew, of course, that Tsin's work could not be undone without his permission. They also knew Blue Jay's words were only intended to gain their favor. He was still filled with arrogance and vanity. They knew he was neither a mighty fisherman or a great hunter. Still, they could not just refuse his request. They would have to let him prove his boasts, and if he could prove them, they would have to grant as much of his request as they could.

"Blue Jay," said one of the shadowy figures at last, "you say you are a great hunter. Does that mean you have superb prowess with the bow and arrow?"

"Indeed it does," replied Blue Jay. "If there is anyone who can best me at archery, I have yet to meet him."

"Very well," declared one of the three ghosts. "We will see how proficient you are by way of a contest. You will match your skills against the supernatural person we call—He Who Guides the Hunters. If you can defeat him in an archery contest, we will be pleased to restore your pleasant voice. We can, however, do nothing about your singing as Tsin alone can restore that."

The four journeyed inland for several hours eventually coming upon He Who Guides the Hunters. He was asked if he would be willing to engage in a contest with Blue Jay, whom the spokesman for the shadowy trio described as "a truly great archer and a mighty hunter."

He Who Guides the Hunters pretended to be very impressed as he agreed to the contest. He expressed doubts that such a contest would be fair to him as he had not hunted for several centuries and was truly out of practice.

Poor Blue Jay fell right into the trap. He was such a braggart that he really believed he was a hunter of great talent. He promised to take it easy on the ghostly archer.

41

It was only when He Who Guides the Hunters began to chuckle to himself that Blue Jay suddenly realized he was being tricked. He suddenly announced he would be unable to enter the contest because he had not brought his bow or any arrows with him. He asked that he be excused from his challenge.

He Who Guides the Hunters replied that he would be pleased to loan Blue Jay his bow and arrows. He told Blue Jay he would be truly saddened if he could not at least attempt to match Blue Jay's skills. Blue Jay, thinking the ghostly being was perhaps not all that skillful, allowed his vanity to mislead him. He agreed to use the supernatural person's bow and arrows.

He Who Guides the Hunters stepped forward. Taking an arrow from his quiver he notched it to the bowstring, drew the string back, took aim at a tree some fifty feet distant, and loosed the arrow. It coursed its way through the misty air, struck the tree, and held fast.

"The arrow," said the ghost, "is the target. The first of us who splits the arrow's shaft is the winner. You, Blue Jay, may shoot first."

Blue Jay once again realized he had placed himself into a fine mess, but was too vain to bring himself to ask forgiveness of the ghosts and beg leave to return from whence he had come. Instead, he accepted the bow and an arrow.

Stepping forward, Blue Jay notched the arrow to the drawstring, took careful aim at the tree, and loosed the arrow. It sped truly to imbed itself in the tree a mere fraction of an inch from the target. Blue Jay began to think he had done very well indeed.

He Who Guides the Hunters then took two arrows, notched them both to the string, drew back, and aimed at the tree. He released them with a flourish and both arrows streaked silently and true. One split the shaft of the target arrow—the other split Blue Jay's arrow.

Blue Jay, seeing the arrows strike, flew away as quickly as he could. The supernaturals, however, sent a falcon after him. The falcon easily outdistanced the hapless Blue Jay, caught him, and carried him back to the ghosts.

"Blue Jay," the supernatural people told him, "you came to us for help but took up our time with stupid boasting. You told us of your great talents when you have none.

"Had you come to us contritely with humility, we would have been pleased to help you. But you came in insolence and that we cannot forgive.

"Because you have displeased us we will punish you by removing your power of speech. From this moment forward you, all your children, and all their children will be unable to speak. We will leave you with but one note.

"That single note, Blue Jay, will be but a piercing screech good only to sound warnings of danger. All of earth's creatures, when they hear you, will remember that you were punished for your great sin of vanity."

With that they dismissed him and ordered him to leave the misty isles. Blue Jay returned in sorrow to Haida-Gwai to live for the rest of time unable to sing even a single note.

From that time forward the Haida people looked upon Blue Jay with scorn and contempt. He became a symbol of misfortune and an omen of bad luck. It was considered a bad sign should a blue jay perch on a lodge pole and screech his raucous warning, so great care was taken to prevent Blue Jay from perching anywhere near the village.

Blue Jay, the Original Stingy Person
A Knight's Inlet Story

In the very early days all of Great Spirit's children shared the same language, had the ability to live together in harmony, and even the animals and birds had human qualities. The animals and birds could walk as did men, and they could build houses and canoes, hunt and fish, and were in no way hindered in the ways they are today. They shared the same villages, and sometimes the village chief was a man and sometimes a bird or an animal. The chief was always chosen for his wisdom, courage, strength, and ability to lead others.

In those days, on the south shore of what is now called Knight's Inlet, there was a prosperous village. It was prosperous because those who lived in it were so brave that no one dared attack them. This allowed the villagers plenty of time to pursue peaceful endeavors. They hunted and fished along the inlet and traded their goods with their neighbors.

Their chief, a human who was very wise, believed kindness was the key to peaceful relations with others. Because of this belief, no traveler who stopped at the village was ever turned away. Food and shelter were always available to anyone who ventured to the village.

One day the chief fell ill and died. The villagers lamented and held a council to determine who should be their new leader. There were several candidates, all of whom had the necessary attributes for the position. The chief's son was too young to be considered, but all agreed that when he reached manhood he would be a likely choice. Beaver was also considered as were Wolf and Whale. Wolf was the choice of many, but he was away for long periods of time during the winter months because he liked to hunt in the north woods. Beaver was considered, but he slept all winter and winter was a time when leadership was greatly needed. Whale was also thought to be a good choice, but he always went to warm southern waters during the cold months and an absentee chief was not suitable. The final choices were Raven and Blue Jay.

Raven, the villagers knew, was very wise and would make an excellent chief, but Blue Jay was stronger and more likely to provide a better defense against any invaders. The vote was close until Blue Jay appealed to the villagers' sense of insecurity when he made a speech and convinced them that strength was extremely important. Raven, in his speech, told the villagers that he would carry on the late chief's idea of kindness toward all. Most of the villagers sided with Blue Jay. In the final vote only the chief's small son voted for Raven.

Blue Jay was elated and set about to be chief with great enthusiasm. At first he did a good job, but toward the end of summer he grew worried that food would be in short supply during the winter. Instead of gathering more, he ordered that no more hospitality be offered to passing strangers. From that day all who called at the village were turned away. Soon, the other villages along the inlet retaliated by refusing to deal with the hunters and fishermen from Blue Jay's village.

Because of this, by the time autumn arrived, the village had nothing except that which the villagers had caught themselves. Raven warned that they should resume trade with the other villages in order to gather different foods. Variety, he warned, was necessary to weather a cold winter.

No one listened to Raven because the villagers all thought Blue Jay was right. They continued to turn away travelers and refused to trade with those who sought them out. No one noticed, but as winter approached the village storehouse contained only smoked salmon and clams. In previous years the storehouse had contained a great variety of foods. The villagers had not realized the extra food had come through trade with others.

By the time winter set in, the villagers were all tired of eating clams and dried salmon. Worse, they were beginning to discover there was a shortage, which meant they would not have enough to last the entire winter. They gathered around Blue Jay and complained loudly to him.

"If you had not been so stingy to others," they cried, "we would not be in this sorry state."

But Blue Jay refused to reconsider his ideas. He merely placed everyone on a ration and told them there would be enough to last the winter. By midwinter, however, the villagers were all very hungry. Even the foolish Blue Jay knew he would have to do something. He called the hunters together.

"Tomorrow," he announced, "we will go in two boats to the big island at the mouth of the inlet and there we will look for seals."

The following morning the canoes were made ready. Just as they were being pushed into the water the former chief's small son appeared on the beach.

"I wish to accompany you to the island," he said. "It is my duty as a future warrior to do so."

"No," Blue Jay replied. "You are too small. You would be in the way."

Raven interceded on the boy's behalf, urging that he be allowed to go with the party, but Blue Jay refused. The boy returned, sadly, to his lodge. Blue Jay and the others then paddled away to the big island. They hunted all day and by afternoon a seal had been netted in shallow water. The hunters were all happy and sang as they began to load the meat into their boats.

"Stop," commanded Blue Jay. "Cook the meat over the fires. We shall eat it here."

Raven objected saying the meat must be shared with all the village. Blue Jay angrily knocked Raven to the ground and once again ordered the meat to be cooked and eaten.

"Only warriors need meat," he said. "Women and children need only clams to survive."

His orders were carried out and the seal was eaten on the island. Blue Jay then told his men to douse the fire and prepare for the return home.

"We shall return here tomorrow morning," he said. "We have found good hunting."

Raven, when he thought no one was looking, retrieved some of the cooked meat and hid it in his boat. But Blue Jay had seen him and when the boats were well out from shore he went to the hiding place in the rear of the boat, took the meat and threw it over the side.

"That meat," complained Raven, "was for the women and children."

"Meat is for men only," retorted Blue Jay. "Women and children can exist nicely on clams and mussels."

Raven said nothing more and returned to his paddling in silence.

The next morning the boats were once more readied for the journey to the island. Once again the late chief's son came to the beach.

"I wish to go with you," he said. "It is my duty to go with you."

As before Blue Jay refused his request. He pushed the boy to one side as he passed. Raven once again spoke up.

"He should come with us, Blue Jay," said Raven. "He is one who may someday be chief. He must learn."

"Someday, perhaps," Blue Jay answered, "but that day is yet to come. Today he is too young and too small."

The boy said nothing. He watched the boats as they departed then walked slowly back to his lodge.

For Blue Jay and his men, the day went much as the first day. The hunters caught another seal. As before, Blue Jay ordered that the meat be cooked and eaten on the spot. Raven once again objected. Blue Jay, as he had the previous day, knocked Raven to the ground. Again Raven tried to smuggle some meat aboard the boat, but Blue Jay again caught him. He threw the meat into the ocean.

"Women and children," he cried, "can live on clams and dried salmon. Only warriors need meat."

So, once again, the boats returned to the village without meat. The women lamented as did the children, but no one told them what Blue Jay had done.

On the third day the boats again were made ready. The little boy again came to the beach, but this time he did not ask to go with the party.

"I will stay here today," he said to Blue Jay. "I have things to do. I have had a dream."

The boy then turned to Raven. "You, oh Raven, were also in my dream," he said. "You also have things to do, but for today you must go to the big island. There you will see an unusual bird."

Having said that the boy turned and walked to his lodge. Raven was puzzled and Blue Jay seemed worried. He wondered what the boy meant and he remained in deep thought all the way to the island.

When the boats arrived at the island the hunters began their search for meat. Blue Jay kept Raven in his group in order to keep a close eye on him. The boy's statement had him worried.

Meanwhile, back in the village, the boy had left his lodge. He walked to a clearing in the woods and there he lit a small fire. Then he sat down on a fallen log to wait. His dream had told him to do that as he was to be visited by a supernatural creature.

He had been waiting only a few minutes when suddenly a large eagle flew into the clearing. The eagle came to within a few feet of where the boy was sitting.

48

"I am known as Greatest Eagle," the great bird announced, "and you must do as I command. I am here as the messenger of Great Spirit. What I tell you I can not repeat so you must listen intently. It is important that you follow my instructions without error."

"I will do as you command," replied the boy.

The eagle instructed the boy to gather roots and herbs which he must place on the fire. He was then to stand in the smoke while turning around slowly exactly four times. This the boy did. The magic in the smoke turned the boy into an eagle. He stood in the clearing waiting for the next command.

"You will now fly to the big island," Greatest Eagle commanded. "You will do nothing there except to remain the entire day perched in a tall tree. Stay in full view of both Raven and Blue Jay. When they prepare to leave you will fly back to your village. When you land you will resume your human form. Talk to no one. Return here tomorrow morning and gather the roots and herbs. Light the fire but do not put the roots or herbs into it. Wait for me and I will come to you with instructions."

Having delivered his instructions, the supernatural eagle flew quickly away. Once he had disappeared from sight the boy also took to the air. He headed directly for the island where he perched on the top branch of a tall tree. He remained there the entire day.

Blue Jay had seen the eagle as it approached and had watched it take its place on the top branch of a tall tree. He watched the eagle all day and wondered why such a bird would stay so long in one place. Although he was curious, he said nothing about the eagle to any of the others. Raven had also seen the eagle and, like Blue Jay, it had made him wonder. For an eagle to spend an entire day in one tree on one branch is unusual.

All day the warriors hunted and for their work they were rewarded with two seals. These they cut up and cooked as Blue Jay had ordered. When the meat was ready they began to eat it. Suddenly a boat with several hunters in it approached the island. The boat was different from any the warriors had ever seen before, and the paddlers wore brighter clothing than was usual for the area.

"Hulloah," the paddlers called. "Will you share with us your meat for we are very hungry?"

Raven was about to invite them ashore when Blue Jay pushed him aside.

"Go away," he shouted to the men in the boat. "We have barely enough for our own use. We can share nothing with you."

The strange paddlers turned their boat around and without another word paddled away to the north. Blue Jay then ordered his men to eat their meat as it was time to return to the village. Raven again told the warriors to place the remaining meat in the boats, but Blue Jay took the meat and threw it into the fire where it burned.

"Meat is for warriors," he repeated. "Women and children can eat clams and mussels."

As Blue Jay spoke those words the eagle lifted silently from his perch in the tall tree. It glided across the heads of the warriors below, then turned and flew in the direction of the village.

"Raven," Blue Jay asked, "did you see the strange eagle?"

"I did see it," Raven replied. "I wonder what it was doing. It is unusual for an eagle to sit so long in one place."

"I wonder if it is a sign?" asked Blue Jay.

"Perhaps," Raven answered. "Did you notice the eagle had feet like a man?"

"Yes," Blue Jay replied. "That is what has me worried."

The trip back to the village, however, was without event so Blue Jay stopped worrying. Raven, however, could not forget the strange bird. He felt it was an omen.

The following morning Blue Jay once again called the warriors together and they departed for the big island. The boats were no sooner out of sight than Greatest Eagle arrived in the clearing. The boy had not yet taken the form of an eagle but had prepared the fire and had gathered the roots and herbs which he would need.

"Again today you will listen to my instructions carefully," commanded the eagle. "I can speak them once only."

"I understand," replied the boy.

The supernatural eagle then told the boy what was expected of him. Greatest Eagle then gave him some magic dust and flew away to the north.

The boy, when the eagle was gone from sight, hurried to the village storehouse where he gathered all the rawhide thongs he could find. Then he returned to the clearing where he placed the roots and herbs on the fire. When the smoke was thick enough he entered it and turned around slowly four times. The magic in the smoke turned him once again into an eagle. Grasping the thongs in his beak he flew as fast as he could to the big island. He arrived at the island long before Blue Jay and his warriors, but he wasted no time. Flying quickly along the shore he dropped the thongs one at a time among the rocks and on the beach. Then he sprinkled the magic dust over the beach. Once that had been accomplished he flew back to the village.

The eagle landed on the beach near the village. He called together all the women and, when they had gathered about him, he told them who he was. He told them about Greatest Eagle and told them to do as he commanded without question.

"You have all suffered too much at the hands of the stingy Blue Jay and from this day forward you will be free of his harsh rule," he told them. "All of you, except Raven's wife, will enter the ocean and swim toward the big island. When you arrive there you will swim around the island four times. Swim close to the shore but do not go onto the land.

"As you complete the fourth circle Great Spirit will change you into whales. You will then proceed into the open sea where you will remain until called upon to return to this land."

The women did as they were commanded. As they waded into the water they were amazed to find the water was not cold to them. They knew the eagle was indeed a magic creature of great power. They proceeded toward the big island.

As the women began to swim away, the eagle told Raven's wife to return to her lodge and there await the return of her husband. Then he called all the children to gather around him.

"You have all suffered from the harsh rule of Blue Jay," he told them, "but from this day forward you will be free from his stingy ways. You will do as I command. You will enter the water

51

and swim toward the big island. Once there you will swim around the island four times. You will approach near the shore but do not go to the land. On your fourth circle Great Spirit will change you into puffins. Then you will take to the air and fly directly to the cliffs of the northern islands. You will remain there until you are recalled to this land."

He then told Raven's children that they must stay in the village with their mother. They went immediately to their lodge.

The other children all entered the water as the eagle had commanded. They, too, were surprised that the water was not cold to them and they knew the eagle was certainly a creature of great magic.

The eagle then called the village slaves together. He told them that from this day forward they were free.

"You will enter the water," the eagle told them. "As you swim away Great Spirit will turn you into sea otters. From this day forward you will be free to go where you choose."

The slaves then entered the water and were turned into otters. They all swam away in pairs in different directions.

The eagle then turned back into human form. The boy walked quickly along the shore laying thongs here and there and sprinkled them with the magic dust. When he was finished he called upon the powers Greatest Eagle had given him. With these powers he destroyed the entire village sparing only the lodge belonging to Raven. This he left intact.

He then returned to his eagle form. Flying directly to the big island he perched once more on the branch in the tall tree. From there he watched the scene below.

The hunters were not enjoying good hunting. They had seen no seals. Blue Jay, knowing there would be no meat, ordered them to dig clams and harvest mussels from the beach but they had been unable to dig clams because the sand proved too hard and their implements could not penetrate it. They also found the mussels would not pry loose from the rocks. The magic thongs and the dust which the eagle had placed on the beach held them firmly in place.

Shortly after the eagle arrived, the warriors spied their women swimming toward the island. They watched helplessly as the women circled the island four times then swam out to sea after they had changed into whales. The warriors began to chant prayers of remorse.

They changed from prayer to wailing songs of anguish when they saw their children swimming toward the island. When, on the fourth circle of the island the children all turned into puffins and departed northward, the cries increased.

Blue Jay could not believe what he was seeing. He ordered the warriors into the boats. They paddled as fast as they could toward the village. As the boats pulled away, Blue jay looked back just in time to see the eagle leave its perch in the tree.

"Raven," said Blue Jay, "I greatly fear the eagle with human feet."

But Raven remained silent. He was beginning to understand what was happening.

When the warriors reached the village they found it deserted. The lodges were all gone as were the women and children. Even the slaves were gone. The men stood in awed silence, confused, not knowing what to do. As they milled about, the eagle alighted and perched in a tree.

"Hear me," the eagle called. "You are being punished for following a false leader who has led you into ways of stinginess and unkind acts. Only Raven has been spared. His family remains with him. His lodge remains intact but he is forbidden to share it with any of you.

"Hear me, oh Raven," the eagle continued. "You are to live in the comfort of your own home with your wife and your children. You are commanded to keep your own counsel. You will extend no aid or comfort to any of these stingy people. You will be advised in good time as to the limits of these prohibitions.

"Hear me, Blue Jay. You are the leader of these foolish and miserable warriors so you will continue to lead them for as long as you are able."

The eagle with human feet then rose on outstretched wings and flew away toward the misty lands of the supernatural creatures.

Blue Jay, very much frightened, turned to Raven for advice, but Raven walked quickly to his lodge. Then Blue Jay ordered his men to gather clams and mussels to cook. As had happened on the island, the mussels would not come free from the rocks or the sands and the clams could not be dug from the sands.

Blue Jay and his warriors spent the rest of the cold winter huddled together in a crude shelter they were able to put together. They ate only shrubs and roots which they managed to find in the woods. From time to time canoes and boats bearing men from other villages would pass, but none ever came over in answer to the calls for help. By the end of the winter the warriors were starving and indeed miserable. They realized they had chosen a bad leader in Blue Jay and they turned against him. He was put to flight and warned never to return.

Raven, meanwhile, kept to himself as he had been ordered. His lodge was dry and warm. Laughter and shouts of happy children sounded from within its walls. Food was not in short supply to Raven. He could venture into the forest and return with enough meat to feed his family. He waited for the sign he knew would come.

Having exiled Blue Jay the warriors turned to Raven for leadership, but he told them he was waiting for the sign from the eagle with human feet. They would have to fend for themselves. So, their misery continued.

One morning while Raven was repairing his fishing nets near the beach the eagle appeared. Raven recognized him at once and greeted him as he would greet a brother. He knew the eagle was really the chief's son. The eagle told Raven that it was time for him to take the mantle of chief and lead his people from their misery.

"The foolish warriors are now fully repentant," the eagle said. "You will now show them the path they must follow in order to return to the graces of Great Spirit.

"They will come to you again," the eagle continued. "They will beg you to become their chief. This time you must accept their pleading. You will lead them in the ways of your own beliefs. They will do as you bid and this village will once again know prosperity. In time the women and children shall return.

"You will rule over them for many years, and when the time comes that you must leave this life, you will go to the land of supernatural creatures. From that time onward you will be known as The Raven Who Rules Wisely."

Then the eagle with human feet departed for the last time.

Raven did indeed become chief. He restored the village to its former prosperity. The villagers were once again smiled upon by Great Spirit as their reputations as generous people became known far and wide. Their wives and children were returned to them.

When, as the eagle had predicted, Raven left the earthly world after many years, he journeyed to the land of supernatural creatures. He was never forgotten by the villagers, and their artisans carved many poles in his honor. Even today, along Knight's Inlet there are villages which show totem poles honoring Raven. He is always near the top, usually just below an eagle with human feet.

6   The Changer

Among the most intriguing legends told by West Coast natives are the stories of the Changer. This powerful god was, with variations, part of nearly every tribe's legends. The Lummi of the Puget Sound area, and the Puyallup of the Salishan group, tell of Kwa'te, which in either language means the Changer. Kwa'te sought out unhappy creatures and changed them into what they really wanted to be or what they would be better suited as being. Kwa'te was not above admitting that even a great spirit might make a mistake now and then. However, Kwa'te did not always change such creatures into what they wanted to be. He would often punish creatures who were evil or vain, selfish or irreverent, dishonest or unkind by changing them into loathsome creatures such as devilfish, toads, or slugs.

Kwa'te traveled among the Lummi to whom he gave the great gift of fire. He was also very kind to the Puyallup in many ways. Puyallup storytellers relate how Kwa'te had married their Frog Princess, the daughter of the powerful Frog Chief and how he took her to live in his home on the moon. The people of the Puyallup tribes could look to the moon when it was full and see Kwa'te walking with his Frog wife. She was easily identifiable by the bundle she carried on her back.

To the Kwakiutl people of Vancouver Island Kwa'te was known as Q'an'iquel'ukwha, the Transformer. He walked about the earth in the company of his brother, W'allus. These two great gods also lived on the moon, and they could be seen when the moon was full. When they traveled on the earth they kept busy changing unhappy creatures into better forms or changing the evil creatures into loathsome forms.

The two kept busy for centuries on Vancouver Island and then Q'an'iquel'ukwha moved into the northern lands of ice and snow to continue his travels. Kwakiutl legend has it that W'allus stayed behind to finish their work on Vancouver Island. W'allus eventually roamed about on the northern tip of the island before going to what is now called Scott Island where he stayed for a long time. Then he went to Calvert Island before returning to the moon where he would stay for all time. They know W'allus went to the two outer islands because there are huge footprints imprinted in the flat rocks on both islands. They say these are W'allus' footprints because W'allus means *big one,* and W'allus was much bigger than his brother, Q'an'iquel'ukwha, even though he was not as powerful in his magic.

Kwa'te is well chronicled also by the Makah and the Quinault people who inhabited the land along Cape Flattery in Washington State. These two tribes got along quite well, but there was obviously enough rivalry, if not animosity, to give rise to one legend told by the Quinault.

Why Kwa'te Gave Dogs to Indian Villages
A Quinault Version

One day when Kwa'te was walking in the woods he came across a pack of wild dogs. These dogs were lean and appeared to be very hungry. The dogs recognized Kwa'te and fell down before him.

"Why are you so poor looking, my wild children?" asked Kwa'te.

"Oh, great Changer!" the dogs cried, "we are very hungry. We have fallen on hard times."

"This is most unusual," mused the god. "I have placed deer in great number in the forest. The streams and the rivers teem with fish of many kinds. The ground is home to small animals

57

which number in the thousands. Why do you not hunt and fish as I intended you to?"

The wild dogs wailed most mournfully and lamented in loud voices.

"Oh, great Kwa'te! We cannot sweep the fish from the water as do the bears because our paws are too small. We are unable to catch the deer because we are neither as fleet of foot nor as strong as the cougars. The small animals elude us because they are agile and can burrow into the ground faster than we can dig. Our claws are not suited for digging."

The dogs continued their wailing while they implored Kwa'te to change them into creatures who were better equipped for life in the forest. Kwa'te thought about the situation for a few minutes. He finally spoke, "It is indeed sad that you cannot properly make your way in my world. Still, I do not wish to change all my wild dogs. I will, therefore, change some of you into human creatures. The remainder will keep your present forms, but I will send them to many different villages where the people will feed and care for you. In exchange for their good treatment you will give them your lasting loyalty as well as guard the villages from strangers who may prowl about with evil in their hearts. This you will do for all time."

Kwa'te then sprinkled magic dust over the dogs which caused them all to fall fast asleep. While they slept Kwa'te summoned the Thunderbird who whisked half of their number away by scooping them up in his great talons.

Thunderbird flew throughout the land leaving two dogs, one male and one female, in each of many villages. He told the people of Kwa'te's wishes and they were pleased to accept the dogs as a gift from Kwa'te. That is why there are dogs in every Indian village even to this day.

The remaining half of the pack eventually awoke from their deep sleep to find they had indeed been changed into human creatures. Kwa'te, however, had left them with many of their former traits. Throughout the years of their existence these people had difficulty hunting and fishing, and they never became truly prosperous. These people are the ancestors of the Makah people.

One must bear in mind the Quinault version of this story is highly prejudiced, as the Makah are no less resourceful or prosperous than other nations. It is not mere coincidence that the Makah tell a similar story about the Quinault.

Why Kwa'te Created Different Languages
A Makah Story

Kwa'te, the Changer, traveled through the rain forests of Washington's northwest coast making changes as he went. He liked the area very much and, because he was never in a hurry to depart, he often stayed for years at a time. One day, however, as he was walking quietly through the woods, a small bird came to him with a message that his wife, the Frog Princess, needed him on the moon. Kwa'te had been working hard and was tired, so he lowered the sky in order that he would not have so far to fly in order to get home.

When Kwa'te reached the moon he was pleased that his trip had been shortened a great deal, so he decided to leave the sky where it was. This was all very well for Kwa'te, but the lowered sky caused a mist to hang heavy and thick over both the land and the waters of Puget Sound. The mist was so thick that the fishermen could not venture far from shore in their canoes, and the hunters were unable to find the deer in the forest. This condition lasted for many weeks so the people called a great council to deal with the problem.

All the people from the entire area journeyed to one place where they discussed the situation. They argued about how they might have the sky raised. They decided to implore Kwa'te to help them. They did not know the Changer had lowered the sky. When he appeared to them in answer to their songs, he told them that he would not raise the sky until he had finished with his work on the moon. Then he left.

The people did not want to wait as they knew Kwa'te might not return for many months. After much discussion they decided that they, themselves, would raise the sky. It was suggested that a huge pyramid be formed by all the people standing on each other's shoulders, the strongest at the base and the smaller at the top. Once everyone was in place, those at the top would give a mighty heave and the sky would be restored to its original height. The plan seemed a good one and the people decided to implement it at once.

It took all the people to form the great pyramid, but the job was soon finished. The sky was raised and the mists cleared away.

Kwa'te, however, had watched the people form their pyramid and he was most displeased. When the sky had been put back into its original location, Kwa'te reappeared to the people. He berated them in an angry voice demanding to know why they had put themselves in his place. The chiefs spoke for the people and as a result Kwa'te, seeing that he had indeed been selfish, agreed to leave the sky in place.

However, he told them he could not tolerate their great insolence in undoing what he had caused to be. He told the people they would have to be punished. Kwa'te then sprinkled magic dust over all the people. When they had all fallen asleep Kwa'te rose into the sky and returned to the moon.

When the people awoke, they all wondered what it was that Kwa'te had done. They all milled around uncertain of what to do next. They all spoke out at once and it was then they knew what the Changer had done. A few hours before all the people had spoken one language, now they spoke many. They were unable to understand each other and found they could not converse with their former neighbors.

They realized that different groups spoke different languages and that only those of their own group could understand what their neighbor was saying. The people then formed into groups according to languages. They all went away to the different parts of the forest.

Thus Kwa'te formed the many tribes each with its own language. The wise elders realized Kwa'te had done this so that never again could all the people assemble to discuss ways of undoing the things that Kwa'te had caused to be or to change anything that he had created.

7   Legends of the Coyote God

About a mile east of Penticton, British Columbia, at the end of a trail winding through scrub brush and sage, there is a clearing in which stands, as it has for thousands of years, an oddity of nature—a balancing rock. Scientists and geologists explain this phenomena by producing data and calculations based on centuries of wind and weather, saying how both combined to erode a once solid column of sandstone into what appears to be a rock perched precariously atop a narrow pedestal.

This scientific explanation may be feasible, but to the native people of the Okanagan Valley, the real explanation is one far removed from mathematical and geologic theories. This unusual sculpting, known locally as Coyote Rock, is the personal handiwork of the all-powerful Coyote God, the greatest of Tyee Sahale's supernatural animals.

Those who have viewed this strange rock with an open mind can understand the Indian belief that this was indeed the work of a god.

Coyote Rock, particularly from a distance of a few hundred feet, looks remarkably like a great wolf seated on his haunches, head thrust skyward as if howling a challenge. The rock is even the same sandy color of the smaller coyotes which are seen from time to time as they prowl among the sagebrush in search of small game. It is even more disturbing when viewed under the pale light of a full moon on a summer night. The viewer is filled with a strange foreboding, a feeling that he is in the presence of ghosts.

Coyote God, who inhabited the valleys of the Monashee Mountains, the Thompson Valley, the Okanagan Valley of British Columbia and Washington

State, the Yakima Valley in Washington State, and several locations in Oregon and Northern California, was the acknowledged leader of the supernatural animals.

These animal gods, according to legend, inhabited the earth long before the arrival of humans. Tyee Sahale, the Great Spirit of the inland natives, was allied with the supernatural animals in the never ending battle against the forces of the evil spirits who also roamed the earth. The evil spirits were very powerful in their own right and Tyee Sahale needed assistance keeping the evil ones in check. Thus, he leaned heavily on the supernatural animals for assistance.

The supernatural animals had human qualities. They could walk upright if they chose to, could talk with each other in a common language, and lived in complete harmony with each other. They formed groups to oppose the evil spirits if the situation demanded or battled the evil spirits in single combat if the need arose.

Their chief purpose was to travel the world putting things in order. Greatest Beaver, for instance, built dams which directed the course of rivers, formed lakes, and caused waterfalls. Greatest Squirrel buried acorns and pine cones in the valleys which in time grew to be the vast forests. All had tasks of importance. But, as powerful as they all were, none had the magic of the Coyote God and they all looked to him for leadership in times of greatest stress and troubles.

The Coyote God roamed the entire range of Tyee Sahale's world. His adventures were many. He saved the world's animals from a great flood which had been caused by an evil spirit who lived in a great lake. The lake involved is always the largest one in the immediate area. The story itself, however, is basically the same.

Coyote God and the Great Flood
An Okanagan Version

The Coyote God was tired from his wanderings and he was

very hungry as well. Also, the evening was growing cool and he longed for the warmth of a fire. Upon arriving at the shore of Lake Okanagan, Coyote God decided it would be a good place to camp for the night. He set aside his bow and magic arrows and began to build a small fire from twigs he collected from a nearby bush. He took his ax from his pack and began to chop the wood he would need for the long night.

Suddenly, an evil spirit rose up from the lake.

"You cannot camp here," the spirit called. "This is my lake. You must leave at once."

"There is room enough for all," Coyote God replied while continuing to cut his wood. "I intend only to spend the night. In the morning I will be on my way."

"You will leave now!" the spirit cried angrily. "I will not allow you to use my lake. It is mine alone."

But Coyote God, ignoring the evil spirit, continued to cut his firewood. This enraged the evil lake spirit. He shouted out magic words in a loud voice which cast a spell upon the lake. The water began to rise at a rapid rate and Coyote God was forced to flee to higher ground. He had barely enough time to retrieve his bow and magic arrows.

When Coyote God had scrambled to the high ground away from the lake the waters receded. Coyote God then returned to the lake's sandy beach, but the minute he stood on the beach the spirit arose once again from the water. This time, however, Coyote God was ready for him and shot the spirit with a magic arrow. Coyote God was never known for great patience where evil spirits were concerned.

The evil one, staggering under the impact of the arrow, fell back into the water. But, just before he went under the waves, he cast another spell upon the lake. The water immediately began to rise.

Coyote God again scrambled up the bank to higher ground. As fast as he ran and as high as he climbed the water continued to rise. He realized the arrow had not killed the spirit outright. He knew the spirit still had power and would be able to keep the water rising until the arrow managed to do its work. Coyote God

knew he had unwittingly unleashed upon the earth a terrible crisis by vexing the evil spirit into a desperate final act.

As Coyote God ran he called out in a loud voice which could be heard throughout the land.

"Run! Run!" he called. "Go at once to the highest mountain where the water cannot reach you."

As he ran, he continued his loud calling until all the animals had heard him. They, too, began to run as quickly as they could toward the highest mountain in the valley. They knew that Coyote God would be able to save them if they followed his directions.

The animals all rushed to the top of the highest mountain and remained there for many days until, at last, the water stopped rising. Then, slowly, it began to recede. Coyote God knew then that his magic arrow had killed the evil one. He eventually led the animals down the mountain and they all returned to their own areas to resume their work.

Coyote God Survives a Challenge
A Nicola Version

With the flood ended, Coyote God resumed his travels throughout the land. After many years had passed he came one day to the place we now call Penticton. In those days there was no village, but the place was well known because it was used as a meeting ground. The word *Penticton* means meeting place. There he was told by a messenger sent from Tyee Sahale that a young wolf, an evil spirit in disguise, had appeared in the land. The messenger informed Coyote God that the newcomer was traveling around telling all who would listen that he would be a better leader than Coyote God.

"The young wolf tells every animal he meets that you grow weak with age," the messenger reported to Coyote God. "He says you have grown faint of heart and no longer possess the sensibilities a leader needs. He claims you have grown forgetful and your mind has become feeble."

Coyote God thanked the messenger and sent him on his way.

Then he sat down to think about the young wolf. Coyote God could not allow this evil upstart to stay among the animals, but he could not merely deny the words the interloper was saying. To make denials would prove nothing and might even convince some of the animals that he was making weak excuses to cover up failings. He knew he had to do something of substance.

Now Coyote God was well aware the young wolf was physically stronger than he, being larger in size and much younger in age. He knew also the wolf, being an evil spirit, had magical powers. But he also knew his young rival lacked one attribute that Coyote God possessed. Over the years Coyote God had gained much wisdom. He decided the only way to defeat the young one was to defeat him with one cunning stroke. He would call upon the wisdom of his years to do this.

Coyote God planned his strategy carefully. Though he gave every indication that he was avoiding the young upstart, in reality he was stalking him, biding his time until he could use his wily cunning and his great magic to his own advantage. He waited until one night when the moon was full and the young wolf was meeting with many of the animals in the clearing where Coyote Rock now stands.

Coyote God, as if by coincidence, wandered into the clearing. He appeared confused and seemed to be lost. The young wolf laughed when he spied Coyote God standing on the fringe of the crowd. Even the other animals seemed confused to see him appear to be so old and tired. They looked at each other and muttered that perhaps the young wolf was right. Perhaps Coyote God had grown too old to lead them, they thought. But none was ready to suggest to Coyote God that maybe it was time for him to step aside for the younger one.

A hush fell over the crowd of animals as Coyote God made his way forward. He seemed unsteady as he walked and he appeared to stagger as he drew near the young one.

"You say to those gathered here that you are greater than I," Coyote God said after a long hesitation.

"It is true," replied the evil one. "I am bigger, stronger, faster, and younger than you. It is time you stepped aside. You are growing senile, you can hardly walk, and you seem to be losing your sense of balance. It is I who should lead the animals."

"I am the leader of the supernatural animals," angrily answered Coyote God. "My magic is not weakened despite my age. I sit in the great council with Tyee Sahale. I will continue to lead the animals."

"All that will soon change," retorted the younger one. "The animals will soon realize that you are past your prime years. They will turn to me and I will become their leader."

While the two talked, the crowd of animals shifted about uncertainly. It seemed to them that Coyote God was indeed acting like the old one being described by the young wolf. Yet none was wanting to believe that Coyote God was really growing too old to remain as leader. The animals began to mutter among themselves once more.

Coyote God heard the muttering and he knew the animals were uncertain. That is exactly how he had hoped they would react. He needed their uncertainty if he was to defeat the young wolf.

"Young wolf," said the old one after a minute or two had gone by, "there is but one way to settle this. The animals themselves must decide for it is they who will be led. Will you agree to a contest that the animals may vote and thus decide?"

The young wolf thought for a moment before replying. "What do you propose, old one?"

"Let us both, in turn, call loudly to the moon," Coyote God proposed. "A leader must possess a loud voice so he may summon his followers from the farthest reaches of the realm. Let the animals decide which of us has the more powerful call. Let them decide for good and all."

The evil upstart took little time to consider the proposal. He knew his voice was louder. He knew it would ring out over the hills and through the valleys. He agreed at once to the contest.

"Let it be so," agreed the young wolf. "Let it be that the animals decide. You, old one, may call first."

"Thank you," Coyote God replied. "You are very kind to your elders. Kindness is a great virtue."

Coyote God moved slowly to a small rise in the center of the clearing. He sat upon his haunches for a long moment as if mustering the little strength he had remaining in his body. Then, taking a very deep breath, he thrust his huge head upwards to the moon and howled. It was a long and mournful howl. But, it was not very loud. He saw the look of victory cross the countenance of the young wolf and was pleased that the evil one had fallen into his trap. Then he stepped back and moved to the edge of the clearing.

The young wolf drew himself up to his full size. He was indeed a magnificent animal. His fur glistened in the moonlight as he made his way quickly to the rise. His muscles rippled as he loped in all his majestic and regal splendor to the top of the rise. His very bearing projected utmost confidence. He stood proudly for a brief moment to survey the assembled animals. He knew in his heart he would soon be their leader. Then he sat down, poised his beautiful body, and thrust his head upward toward the moon. He opened his mouth to begin his howl.

Before he could make a sound, however, Coyote God stepped forward. He used his great supernatural powers to cast a spell upon the young wolf and the wolf instantly turned to solid stone. He had not uttered a single sound. Coyote God turned to the animals who looked on in awe and surprise.

"What kind of leader would the young wolf have been?" Coyote God asked the crowd. "He is big, strong, young, ambitious, and powerful. He has powers of magic and may even possess some intelligence, but he lacks wisdom and cunning." Coyote God paused to give the animals a moment to think about what he said.

"Had the wolf been wise," Coyote God continued, "he would never have allowed himself to be tricked in such a way. A wise leader would never fall into such a trap. Those who lack wisdom fill their minds with self-praise and soon fall victim to their own false ideas of what portrays importance. The evil one was easily tricked because he had already fallen into the abyss of self-deception. Leaders cannot allow themselves to be so easily deceived.

"If the young wolf's magic is greater than mine as he claimed, he will have no trouble returning himself to his natural form. If his magic is not as great, he will remain here in this clearing for all time as a memorial to one who let vanity overcome good sense.

"Until the young wolf can return to his proper form, I, the Coyote God, will remain your leader. I will continue to sit in great council with Tyee Sahale."

Whereupon Coyote God gave forth a mighty howl, the likes of which had never before been heard in the world, and the animals thereafter realized he was as powerful as he had ever been. Then, Coyote God led the animals away from the clearing back along the trail to the valley.

The young wolf never undid the magic spell cast upon him by Coyote God. He remains to this day set in stone, poised to begin his great howl to the moon. To this day no sound has come forth.

The Coyote God, to many of the interior tribes, was the supreme supernatural creature second only to their deity Tyee Sahale (or sometimes Kwa'te the principal god of many of the tribes living along the Washington and Oregon coastal regions).

The Chinook society embraced dozens of tribes, many of which are now extinct. Several, like the Multnomah, were wiped out in a sudden and savage epidemic of smallpox brought upon these unfortunate people by visiting sailors who are believed to have traded blankets infested with the smallpox virus to the unsuspecting natives. The Multnomah had no immunity to this ravishing disease.

Although the sailors were probably unaware the blankets were infested, it is known that in more than one instance, unscrupulous traders deliberately sold or traded such blankets to native people then returned to retrieve the blankets and whatever else was collectible after the disease had ravished the village. They would then journey to another area and repeat their terrible crime.

Before the coming of the white man, the Chinook society was an economic empire that extended from the Columbia River Valley, throughout the Thompson Valley down the Okanagan Valley into the valleys to the south as far as northern California. The Chinook were intertribal traders who brought their commerce to all regions of the Pacific Northwest.

The language, of Penutian linguistic stock, varied only slightly from tribe to tribe and was the root language of such important tribes as the Maidu, Wintun, Yohuts, Costonoan, and possibly Miwok. The Penutian family of the Oregon territory included the Coos, Alsea, Kalapuya, and Takelma. Other prominent members of the Penutian group were the Cayuse, Klamath, Yuma, and Walla.

While the Chinook were not, strictly speaking, of the coastal tribes, as the vast majority of their people lived inland, they were well enough acquainted with the coastal tribes to know their customs. The Chinook knew of Raven and Thunderbird and included them in their legends and rituals, but, because of their inland habitat, it was natural for them to consider the coyote as being a symbol of a powerful god from the past.

The coyote represented the enviable possession of fleetness of foot, ability to hunt, and to move among the sage and rocks almost invisibly. The coyote was seen as possessing a high degree of cunning. He was known to be resourceful and able to survive even the harshest of conditions. Because the coyote was so familiar to these natives, and because he seemed to be blessed with all the attributes an animal could ever hope to have, it was natural the early natives would see him as being a supernatural creature.

Coyote in the very early days, it was thought, was the personal messenger of Great Spirit just as the mighty Thunderbird was the messenger of the coastal Indians' gods. The Waso people of northern California called Coyote God Itopolos and considered him a prophet of great vision and foresight. One Waso legend pictures the Coyote God bringing a message from the Great Spirit warning the Waso to expect a strange race of pale people.

These people, Itopolos warned, would arrive in huge wooden canoes that had white wings. Others of the strange race would soon arrive by land. Still later more of the pale people would come in birds made of metal. Itopolos warned the Waso that these pale ones would carry long sticks that spoke like thunder and which would kill anyone the holder pointed the stick at. These pale people, the god warned, had evil magic which caused sickness and death. They cooked their meat in metal kettles. They carried little wooden sticks which produced fire when struck against stone.

From this prophecy the Waso learned about ships, rifles, kettles, smallpox, and matches long before any of them would ever see or encounter white men. The Waso people knew these things would come to pass because Itopolos had told the shamans about it long ago. It is little wonder that a god with such powers would pass his prowess to his descendants. Thus the coyote was considered to be the symbol of the original, all-powerful Coyote God.

Coyote God was revered—but not worshipped—as a deity. The Indians worshipped no deity. Not even Tyee Sahale (the name means Chief Who Lives in the Sky) was worshipped. The Chinook religion, based as it was on nature, taught that all things were part of nature and were therefore equal. Nothing, not even a god, could have ultimate magic or unlimited powers.

Thus, Tyee Sahale, being limited in power, was often forced to call on lesser gods for assistance. That he called on Coyote God more often than others was only because Coyote God's magic was so powerful that the two, when allied in a common cause, were generally enough to defeat any number of evil spirits. According to the myths which have survived the span of time, the alliance of Tyee Sahale and Coyote God was the main force against the evil ones throughout most of the earliest years of the world.

Tyee Sahale Creates the First Humans
A Chinook Story

Tyee Sahale decided to place humans on the earth. He knew what they would look like as he had formulated in his mind how they would appear. He first tried to mould them from dust but an

72

evil spirit came along in the disguise of a wind and blew the humans away. So Tyee Sahale tried to form the humans from water but the water would not hold a shape. Tyee Sahale called out for the Coyote God.

When Coyote God arrived Tyee Sahale told him what he had tried to do. He asked Coyote God if he could offer some advice. Coyote God thought about the problem for some time. Then after he had thought awhile he took from his pouch a magic arrow. He shot it into the ground some distance away. Then he took a magic arrow from Tyee Sahale's pouch and fired it into the shaft of the first arrow.

Tyee Sahale then breathed life into the arrows and removed one from the shaft of the other. He sprinkled the two arrows with magic dust and they became the first man and the first woman.

Tyee Sahale then sent to the man and woman the great Thunderbird who told the pair to journey together, to populate the world and to live by the laws of Tyee Sahale.

Thunderbird told them to call upon Coyote God when they needed advice. Thus were the first Chinook people made.

The Five Wolves and the Supernatural Bears
A Chinook Story

As the years passed the humans which Tyee Sahale and the Coyote God had together created became numerous. As their numbers increased their village became crowded, so they moved away from each other to form other villages. More years passed and soon the valley in which they lived became crowded. It was decided that many of the people should move away from the valley and settle in places some distance away. This idea was deemed by the shamans to be good and some of the people were sent out to find new valleys in which to live.

The people went out but within a few days they returned, complaining they had no way of knowing where they were going. They did not want to go to the lands of North Wind because it was too cold. They feared getting lost in the lands of the great trees near the great salt water. They needed a way to guide themselves through the land so they could make their way back when they had found a fine new valley.

The shamans met in council and discussed the matter among themselves. However, they could not find the answer to the problem. At last it was decided to call to Tyee Sahale for his advice.

Tyee Sahale heard their songs of praise and sent to them a Thunderbird who heard the shamans' complaints about the travelers having no way of knowing which way they were going in their search for new valleys.

The Thunderbird, impatient at the best of times and with no patience for humans at any time, told the people that Tyee Sahale had ordered Sun to travel by day from the high mountains in the east to the ocean in the west. Thunderbird told the people they could not lose their way if they could remember to keep Sun at their left hand when walking or canoeing toward the salt sea, and to keep Sun at their right hand when walking or paddling toward the great mountains to the east. He told them they should keep Sun to their back if traveling toward the land of the North Wind, and to face Sun when traveling to the lands of South Wind.

That, argued the shamans, was all very well for the daylight hours but would do them no good at all when night travel became necessary. How, they asked of Thunderbird, could they be guided at night? Thunderbird replied that only fools and idiots walked in the forests at night. He told them to stay in their camps at night and so avoid meeting the evil spirits of darkness along the way.

But the shamans pursued the issue by stating that many of the people, especially hunters, often had to travel at night and had become lost because there was no sign to guide them.

Thunderbird told the shamans that he had been sent to inform them of the travel signs for daylight use. He had not been told that he must discuss night travel as well.

"I," said Thunderbird, "have given you good advice and am not about to solve your problems of walking about foolishly in the dark."

With those words he left the shamans standing alone in the council house.

The shamans once again called to Tyee Sahale for help. He answered their call by sending Raven who listened and then told them much the same as had Thunderbird.

"I would advise you all to stay within your villages and camps at night," Raven said to them. "Night walking is unsafe because the evil spirits of darkness may capture you in the dark."

He promised, however, to tell Tyee Sahale of their wishes. Then Raven flew away, muttering to himself about how foolish humans were becoming.

Tyee Sahale, because he felt much more regard for his humans than did either Thunderbird or Raven, thought the humans' request had some merit. He decided he would put new stars in the sky which would show the humans how to determine directions while traveling at night. He then called on Coyote God for his thoughts.

"I wish to place some new stars in the sky which will guide my humans at night," he told Coyote God. "I need some of your magic to make this come about."

"Humans should stay inside their lodges during the night," declared the supernatural animal. "They are poorly suited for such ventures. However, I will help if I can."

"It pleases me that you will help," said Tyee Sahale. "I wish to place a bright star into the sky which will show them the northern limits of their lands. But I require also some lesser stars which will point the way to the bright star. Putting the bright star into place will use up much of my magic. If I also place the smaller stars into place, I will have no magic left for a very long time. I cannot afford to use all my magic as I must remain powerful at all times in order to keep the evil spirits at bay. Should they learn I am without magic, they will cause much mischief upon the world."

Coyote God promised to think about the proposal. He said he would return in a few days. He then returned to the earth where he called upon five wolves who were his very good friends. The wolves were brothers and all were very old. Their time on earth was close to being over but Coyote God did not want to lose his good friends to the Spirit of Death. He called on his friends and spoke to them.

"I wish to reward you, my five dearest friends, with immortality," Coyote God said to the five wolves. "It is my wish to place you all high in the night sky where you will remain for all time. You will be seen from earth forever. I will place you so the people of earth may use your light to guide their way in the darkness. May I do that for you?"

The five brothers talked about the idea before agreeing. They all knew their time on earth was short and that it would be good to be immortal. The eldest brother, however, was very wise.

"I am concerned," he told Coyote God, "that eternity might became tedious if we have nothing to do."

"You are right, my oldest friend," replied Coyote God. "I know that being in the sky forever with nothing to do is not a good idea. I will think on this."

Coyote God thought for many minutes. Finally he spoke.

"You will continue to hunt, for hunting is your life and your joy. There are two supernatural creatures—a mother bear and her son—in the sky. I will place you where you can pursue them forever. I will place you far enough from them that you will never be able to overtake them as they are supernatural bears and would tear you to pieces should you get too close and catch them. Is that idea to your liking?"

"Indeed it is," the five cried at the same time. "The idea of forever being hunters is most appealing."

The very next morning Coyote God gathered many arrows and breathed magic into them. Then he shot one high into the sky where it stuck. He then shot a second arrow into the shaft of the first. He placed a third into the second arrow's shaft. He continued in this manner all day and by nightfall he had built a ladder of magic arrows.

That night Coyote God and the five wolf brothers climbed the magic ladder until they reached the top. There, Coyote God and the wolves said good-bye to each other. The Coyote God was just about to leave when he noticed a tiny wolf hurrying up the ladder. The wolves also saw the tiny one.

"It is my tiny grandson," said the elder brother. "Will you also make him immortal? I will keep him safe beside me always."

"I will make it so," agreed Coyote God. They waited for the little wolf to gain the top rung of the ladder, "I will agree if you promise never to allow the little one to venture from your side."

"I do indeed promise," replied the eldest brother. "I will see to it that he stays at my side for all time."

"Good-bye, my dearest friends," Coyote God called out for the final time as he prepared to descend the magic ladder. "Remember, do not approach the bears too closely. You must always let them stay a safe distance away."

"We promise to do as you command," they all replied.

The four younger brothers began to creep toward the two bears. They stopped at the same moment the two bears turned to look at them. Then the oldest wolf, his tiny grandson at his side, moved to a close, but safe, distance and stopped.

Coyote God, seeing the wolves were all in position, fixed them in place with his great magic. He then began his descent of the magic ladder removing the arrows as he climbed down. As he removed each arrow he threw it aside and these arrows stayed in the sky for all time as streaks of light which can still be seen now and then as they travel through the night sky on never ending travels.

When he had once again returned to earth Coyote God looked up into the sky. He could easily see his five good friends and the tiny grandchild and was pleased with his work. The wolves were now in the sky forever. He had assured them immortality.

To this day the five wolves and the tiny grandson can be seen in the night sky as they stalk the two supernatural bears. The five wolves are in a slightly curved line. The three older brothers trail the two youngest. The eldest brother is in the middle and his tiny grandson stands beside him. He is very small and, except on clear nights, is hard to see. He looks as if he is hiding behind his brave grandfather's front leg while peeking out to see if all is safe.

The two bears are directly in front of the five wolves. The mother bear stands above her son. They seem to be facing the wolves as if unsure of whether to flee or to stay and fight. The wolves remain in the stalking position so not to get too close.

After Coyote God had returned to earth he went to Tyee Sahale and told him what he had done. He was pleased that Coyote God had honored the wolves in such a way. He then called forth his great magic and placed a bright star in the sky high in the northernmost region of the sky. Tyee Sahale then sent the Thunderbird once more to the people of the earth.

"Hear me, foolish humans," roared the awesome Thunderbird. "Those of you who are such imbeciles that you would wander in the forests at night will no longer become lost. Remember always to look into the night sky where you will see five wolves and a little one as they stalk two bears. Find the bears and you will see they point in a direct line to the brightest star in the northern sky. That light Tyee Sahale has put there for all time, and it tells you that below it lies the lands of North Wind, the spirit of winter. By its position you will be able to find your way home."

Thunderbird, muttering to himself about the foolishness of humans who would risk wandering about in the darkness, then flew back to his home in a cave atop the highest mountain in the world.

The people, however, did not forget Thunderbird's warnings about the spirits of the darkness. They would venture away from their lodges and villages after dark only when travel was unavoidable, but those who did venture out always felt safer when they could see the wolves stalking the bears.

The stars intrigued the Pacific Indians just as they had all other societies throughout the world. The star group the ancient Greeks named Orion the Hunter to the Chinook was two canoes, each represented by three stars. The canoes point to a smaller star—a supernatural salmon.

The upper three stars depict the canoe of Cold Wind, the spirit who brought winter storms to the earth. The lower three stars depict the canoe of Southwest Wind, the spirit which brought warm weather and who, on occasion, warmed the winter days with the chinook wind. The smaller star, the supernatural salmon, is the prize for which the two spirits compete. The following story tells why the two canoes appear to be racing after the salmon.

Why Two Winds Chase a Salmon
A Chinook Story

In the very early days of the world Southwest Wind took human form and became a great fisherman. He always caught many salmon and his family was well fed at all times. Cold Wind also took human form but was not a good fisherman. Cold Wind was never able to catch enough salmon to feed his family. The reason for this was Cold Wind's habit of always arriving late in the year after most of the salmon had gone.

One day Cold Wind stole some salmon from Southwest Wind's smoke house. He was sneaking away with a large sack of salmon when he was caught by Southwest Wind.

The two began to fight. They wrestled for many days until Cold Wind managed to escape and run away to his canoe. Southwest Wind, exhausted, was forced to give up the chase.

Tyee Sahale, however, had watched the fight with great interest. He decreed that from that day forward Southwest Wind would always defeat Cold Wind. Tyee Sahale then created the seven stars which he placed in the sky. Six appear as if in a race to reach the seventh, the salmon, which represents the prize.

Tyee Sahale did this in order that his decree that Southwest Wind would always defeat Cold Wind would be known for all time by all creatures. He placed Cold Wind's canoe of stars some distance to the rear of Southwest Wind's canoe of stars. Cold Wind's canoe can never catch Southwest Wind's canoe so he will never be able to capture the salmon.

8 Why the Tides Change

A Capilano Story

In the beginning of the world, before the coming of the humans, the supernatural animals held dominion over the land and the sea. Each group of animals had been given control over various parts of the world. Eagle controlled the sky; Salmon controlled the streams; Whale held jurisdiction over the ocean. Cougar held suzerainty over the southern forest and Bear was the king of the northern forests. Great Spirit gave to Beaver the vast responsibility of creating lakes and telling the rivers which way to flow. Squirrel had been given the task of keeping the forests filled with trees. All animals had a part in the orderly management of Great Spirit's world.

To the Wolves Great Spirit gave control of the ocean tides. He told them to keep the tides moving so that sometimes they were at a high level and sometimes they were at a low level. He told the Wolves that he wanted the beaches to be dry at times so that the Raccoons could gather clams and mussels for food.

The Wolves did as Great Spirit had ordered for many years, but on occasion, they would grow lazy and forget to change the tides. The water then either covered the beaches for long periods of time or was low for so long the beaches dried out. Such neglect always caused great hardship for the Raccoons.

Then, one spring, Wolf Chief announced that the tides would not be changed. He told all who inquired that the decision had been made because the fishing was always better when the tide was at the highest level. Wolf people, he said, needed many fish and the best way to get them was to keep the water high.

This decision was denounced by Raccoon Chief who went to Wolf Chief to complain.

"We beseech you," said Raccoon Chief, "to restore the tides to their natural ways. With the beaches covered as they are, my people cannot gather clams and mussels. We will all starve very shortly."

Wolf Chief listened to Raccoon Chief but then he answered very abruptly, "Great Spirit gave the Wolves power over the tides. He told us to lower the water from time to time, but he did not say we had to do it often or on a regular basis. Great Spirit left it to us to change the tides as we pleased. It pleases us to keep the water deep as it helps us in our fishing."

Once again Raccoon Chief implored Wolf Chief to reconsider and once again the request was refused.

"I will lower the tides enough that your people can gather mussels from the rocks," he conceded.

"We cannot live on mussels alone," replied Raccoon Chief. "We must also have clams. Without the clams we shall perish."

Wolf Chief, however, would not relent. Raccoon Chief then left for his own village in great despair. When he arrived home he called a meeting and told the people what had happened. The people then gathered about the council fire and sang songs of lament and sorrow. They felt there was no hope left for them.

As his people sang their songs, Raccoon Chief sat alone in silence at the edge of the clearing. He remained for many hours in deep thought.

At last, when the morning sun was about to reawaken the earth, Raccoon Chief spoke to his people, "Hear me, my people. The women shall at once set to weaving for me a burying basket. When it is made, place me in it after dressing me in my finest robes of bark cloth. Place on my head the finest feathers. Then the warriors shall carry me to the burying grounds. Leave me there alone with only my knife beside me. While the women are preparing the burying basket, messengers shall venture to all the villages to announce my death so all the chiefs will come to pay respects as is the custom."

"How will that help us?" asked the people.

"You will see in good time," replied Raccoon Chief. "It is better that no one know at this time. Now, prepare me for my funeral while the messengers go out with the news."

The Raccoon people hastened to do their chief's bidding. A burial basket was woven, and scouts went out into the camps of the other people in the great forest. As they traveled they loudly lamented the death of their beloved chief. When the basket had been woven the women prepared the chief by dressing him in his finest robes made of bark cloth. They adorned him with the bright feathers which denoted his rank. They placed his finest knife at his side after they had laid him in the basket. Then six of the strongest warriors carried him to the burial ground just outside the village and left him there. The Raccoon people then returned to the village where they sang the songs of lament and the women wailed the verses of sorrow for the departed.

As was the custom, the chiefs of all the nearby tribes came to pay their respects to the dead chief. The last to arrive was Wolf Chief. He stood for some minutes near the basket looking at Raccoon Chief and thought how truly regal the dead chief looked. Wolf Chief admired the fine robe and the bright feathers. At last, he turned to leave.

As Wolf Chief turned, Raccoon Chief leaped from the basket. In his hand was the knife, its blade flashing in the sunlight. With one swipe, the sharp blade sliced off Wolf Chief's tail. He danced about in great pain as Raccoon Chief, holding the tail firmly in his grasp, ran to the fire which blazed nearby. He held the tail above the hot coals.

"Wolf Chief," he called, "I will return your tail to you in an exchange for a treaty on the tides."

"Return my tail," howled Wolf Chief. "You have stolen my magnificent tail. You are guilty of great treachery."

Wolf Chief moved toward Raccoon Chief intending to forcibly retrieve the tail, but quickly stopped when Raccoon Chief shouted a warning.

"Stop, oh Wolf Chief. If you approach closer, I will drop your tail into the coals where it will be destroyed. Stay where you are and we will speak of tides and treaties and clams and mussels."

Wolf Chief knew he was at the mercy of Raccoon Chief. All his magic was in his tail. Without it he was powerless. Wolf Chief sat very still and listened as Raccoon Chief spoke.

"Great Spirit," began Raccoon Chief, "gave to your people the power to control the tides just as he gave to the Eagle and Bear and Raccoon peoples certain powers. He did this to keep his world in order. He gave these powers with the understanding that his children would share with each other the good things of the world. These powers were not given to be used for the selfish advantage of any single animal. Great Spirit ordered all things be shared."

Wolf Chief, hearing the words, sat in silence for some time. At last he spoke, "You are wise, oh Raccoon Chief, and you speak the truth. I feel greatly ashamed for it is indeed true that Great Spirit intended the powers he gave be used for the benefit of all his creatures."

He paused for another minute before continuing. "I will command my people, the Wolf people, to return the ocean to the low water mark. May I now have back my beautiful tail?"

"Wolf Chief," retorted Raccoon Chief, "a return to the low water mark will do no good at all. If the ocean remains there, new clams and mussels will be unable to arrive on the beach. Those already there will not last long, and without replacements, we Raccoons will be no better off than we are now. Also, your people will have difficulties in their fishing.

"We must share in the proper way. Part of the day the water must be deep so your fishing will be good and new clams and mussels will be brought forth from the ocean floor to the shore. Part of the day the water must be low so my people can harvest those clams and mussels."

Wolf Chief was also very wise. He knew Raccoon Chief was right. He spoke so all around could hear his words.

"Hear me all people, Wolf, Raccoon, Eagle, Bear, and all the others of the forest and ocean, so you will all know that from this moment forward the ocean shall flow to its highest level each day where it shall remain for six hours. Then it shall retreat to its lowest level where it shall remain for six hours. So that no one will be trapped by the tide as it comes and goes, it will travel slowly. Each journey will take six hours to complete and it will be so for all time."

Upon hearing those words, Raccoon Chief went to Wolf Chief and, using his magic powers, replaced the magnificent tail to its proper place.

"It is with much gladness in my heart that I return to you, my brother, your beautiful tail," said Raccoon Chief. "I am sorry that the heat from the coals has singed it so that now the tip is darkened."

Wolf gazed on his tail for a moment. Instead of being angry he seemed pleased.

"In fact, my brother," he replied, "it is now even more beautiful than before. The black tip is truly regal and I am so pleased that I will bequeath this mark to all wolves for all time."

"Indeed," he continued, "the smoke from the fire has also altered you and, like me, you look more elegant now than you did before."

Raccoon Chief, curious, rushed to a pool of clear water which was nearby. Looking into it he, too, was pleased with what he saw. The smoke from the fire had darkened his face and it had formed a black mask around his eyes. Like Wolf Chief he was so pleased with his looks that he bequeathed the new markings to all his people.

To this day all raccoons have black masks around their eyes. To this day all wolves have tails with black tips.

The Raccoon people and the Wolf people from that day forward remained on peaceful terms. Never again were there troubles between them. The agreement the two chiefs made that day remains unaltered. That is why the tides ebb and flow from low mark to high mark each day on an endless schedule.

9 The Raven
A Quinault Version

Before the arrival of the humans the world was inhabited only by the supernatural creatures, the magical animals. Kwa'te, the Great Spirit, decided one day to place human creatures on the earth. He had given the matter much thought and designed the humans in such a manner that their survival depended on their ingenuity and viability. He had, however, withheld powers of great magic. His humans, Kwa'te decided, would have to learn skills in order to survive. He had been convinced of the wisdom of this by Thunderbird who did not like the idea of humans in the first place. Thunderbird feared that giving great magic to humans would be harmful to the animals, many of whom were small and helpless.

Kwa'te called together in a great council all his supernatural creatures in order to hear their opinions of his idea. The gathering was held in a meeting place on the shores of what we now call Puget Sound in Washington State. The meeting place has long since grown over with trees and bushes, but there are still some places that can be found along the shoreline which look like they might have been clearings used for meetings of large crowds a long time ago.

Kwa'te told the supernatural animals of his intentions. He described his new creatures and said he would name them Quinault which means *the people*. The animals all listened intently and all wanted to speak when Kwa'te asked for their thoughts. He promised to abide by the majority decision.

Each of the animals offered a point of view. Some were in favor of the humans while others were not. Blue Jay spoke in favor because he wanted new victims for his foolish pranks. Salmon, however, feared the humans would eat all his cousins. Beaver worried that humans, if their numbers became many, would cut down all the trees to make lodges. Squirrel wondered if humans in great numbers might not gather all the acorns and nuts thereby depriving his cousins of their main diet.

One by one the animals spoke. But Raven remained silent. He sat perched on a limb in a nearby tree listening to all the arguments. Yet, he said nothing. Kwa'te, noting Raven's silence, asked why he had not spoken. All the animals turned to look at Raven.

Raven then spoke. He chose his words carefully, "You have all spoken and have set forth your views and concerns. Great Spirit has answered your questions and you seem to be in agreement that placing humans on the earth is a good idea. I agree with Kwa'te when he says we have little to fear from the humans. Still, I have great doubts about some of the suggestions you have made."

He paused awhile to gather his words. He did not wish to offend anyone, least of all Kwa'te. "Kwa'te has assured you that nuts will continue to grow in abundance so there will always be enough for all who would harvest them. Therefore, Squirrel's cousins will never go hungry and will prosper.

"Great Spirit has promised Beaver that trees will always grow in the forests so no shortage will occur. He has extended to Blue Jay the right to torment humans with his foolish pranks. He has promised to endow Salmon with the powers to increase the numbers of his lesser cousins because the humans will depend on fish for food.

"So you all agree that humans should be placed upon the earth where they can gather nuts, build lodges, and fish for food. That is good and I agree.

"Yet I fear that in time the humans will grow very powerful and vain, for Kwa'te plans to give them a great deal of intelligence which, I fear, they will not always use wisely. I fear they will begin to think of themselves as being more important than all others. Then they will come to see themselves as being greater than any of us, instead of being part of our family. This I fear."

Raven said nothing more, and after a few minutes Kwa'te spoke, "Raven speaks with great wisdom and I hear his words. But, his fears are without just cause. I intend to make laws for the people to follow. They will be guided by the laws which I, Kwa'te the Changer, the greatest of all spirits, will proclaim."

"And what, oh Kwa'te," asked Raven, "will you do if the people choose not to obey your laws?"

"They will obey me, oh Raven," Kwa'te replied. "My laws will be enforced by Thunderbird. The people will know that to displease me will bring about my wrath. And my wrath will be visited upon them through Thunderbird."

"Very well," replied Raven. "I know well the great power of Thunderbird and I know the people will greatly fear him. I still have grave doubts that the humans will be long on this earth before they fall upon evil ways, but I will vote with those who approve their coming."

So the supernatural animals voted and it was decided to allow humans to come upon the earth. Some time later, the animals sat again in council with Kwa'te to decide how the earth might be made more hospitable for the newcomers. They spoke of many things and decided that certain changes should be made.

Raven listened to the discussion and, as before, remained silent. It became obvious to all that Raven remained uneasy. His uneasiness was seen by Kwa'te and the other animals. Kwa'te asked Raven why he was still not at ease.

"Oh, great Kwa'te," replied Raven, "I fear my brothers, in their kind thoughts toward these humans which none yet know, have suggested changes which will not be to anyone's benefit. The changes suggested will indeed make the lives of the humans easier, but in their zeal to make the newcomers welcome they are not considering certain—and important—things."

He stopped talking long enough to hop to a lower branch so all in the clearing could hear his words.

"My brothers," Raven began, "you have decided to make the humans welcome in the world and to that I agree for it is good to be kind. But in your kind thoughts you have not considered that these human creatures will soon multiply in numbers greater than yours. This they will do because Kwa'te has granted them a long span of life. In your kindness toward them you speak of making their lives easy. This you intend to do by making changes to the rivers and streams.

"You intend to cause the rivers to flow in such a way that salmon and other fish would be available all year around. If you carry out this plan the rivers will flow to the mountains as well as to the sea. In this way fishing will be made easy for the humans.

"You would have streams and rivers which now flow over the waterfalls to turn instead and flow back to whence they came. In this way the trout will remain in great numbers and fishing will be easy for the humans.

"To these ideas I advise great caution because, if you cause the streams and rivers to flow in all directions, the fish will be unable to complete the lengthy journey that Kwa'te ordained for them long ago. Those in the streams could only return to the mountains when the waters turn. Those in the great salt ocean would be unable to return to the streams of the great beginnings. This would mean the salmon could not spawn and thus the cycle would be denied."

Raven paused in his speech for a moment which gave Greatest Salmon a chance to interject some of his own thoughts. He had been thinking of the difficulties encountered in the journey to the spawning streams, such as the need to swim against powerful currents and the necessity of climbing high waterfalls, and he thought of how easy it would be on his cousins if they could bypass such obstacles. .

"I agree with Raven that turning the streams back at the waterfalls may not be a good idea as it would indeed deny the salmon a way to reach the sea, but I like the idea of rivers which flow in both directions. Such a plan would make my people's return journey very easy."

Raven, still perched above the group, nodded his head, then continued, "Greatest Salmon is quite correct. Rivers flowing in many directions would indeed make the journey easier for Salmon's cousins. It would truly cause fishing to be easy for the humans. But, if the journey and the fishing is made easy there will be great and serious consequences. Hear me, oh my brothers.

"First, all the salmon will be able to complete the journey to the spawning streams, including those of poor quality and those with bad traits of character. The strongest will no longer be the only ones to spawn, and thus will the entire family of salmon be weakened. Soon, the streams and rivers will teem with sickly, weak salmon.

"Those of poor character will choose not to go to the great salt ocean at all because they will be too lazy to make the journey. These weak salmon will remain in the streams where they will grow to size. They will devour the foods upon which the returning salmon depend. The salmon which return at last to the streams will find them barren of nourishment and thus will not be able to sustain their strength for the journey.

"Within a few generations the streams will be filled with such fish—all weak and spindly. In a few more generations no salmon at all will survive for they will not have the will or the strength to survive.

"Then, when all the fish have gone," Raven continued, "the humans will have no fish to eat. Then they will indeed turn to the berries and nuts of the forests' plants and trees. They will turn to the birds and animals and soon thereafter all of our cousins, whom we are supposed to protect and represent at the great councils, will cease to exist. Where, then, will we all be?

"I say to you this: keep the rivers and streams flowing downward to the sea and to the lakes below the mountain peaks. Make room for backwaters and eddies and deep pools where the fish can hide during their journeys. Do not cause the rivers to turn at the waterfalls, so only the strongest can surmount the obstacles. The strong will survive and the strain will not be weakened.

"Let the salmon continue in their difficult journeys so the strong alone will survive. The weak ones will falter and will be caught by the humans.

"Let there be deep pools where the salmon can rest and some can be caught by the humans. Cause the rivers and streams to pass through areas where humans cannot easily go. There the bears may fish unhindered.

"You must not make life easy for the new creatures. They must be made to work for their livelihood. Let them earn their way in Kwa'te's world. Let them use their minds to learn their own way to success.

"Make these things so and the humans, if they are strong and able, will be assured of survival as will all the creatures of the world."

Raven then flew back to his higher perch and looked down on the group as his speech was discussed. As he sat there a tiny wren perched beside him.

"I feel," mused the wren, "that you fear the coming of the humans."

"Indeed, my tiny cousin," Raven replied, "I have a great misgiving stirring within my heart."

"I, too, fear they will prove disappointing to us all," spoke the wren. "I will not put trust in them. I will spread my magic throughout my family so no wren will ever trust a human completely. When they approach, my children will fly quickly away. It will be so for all time."

"You are indeed wise, small one," Raven agreed. "It will be unwise for small birds to trust such large creatures."

After some time had passed, Eagle, who was in charge of the gathering, took his place atop a large rock. He called for silence.

"Raven is our wisest brother," he began. "He has spoken with great wisdom and we have listened. His wise words have reached our ears. It is only right that the humans should not have too easy a life. It is only just that they should be required to earn their share of Kwa'te's world.

"It shall remain for all time that the rivers and streams shall flow from their highest points and seek only the lowest levels. Rivers and streams shall flow to lakes and seas and greater rivers. It will always be thus."

Then Kwa'te spoke. He told the Council that he would heed their wishes. Then he called out magic words. He then gave to Raven some magic dust.

"Raven is indeed the wisest of the supernatural creatures," Kwa'te said to the gathering. "His words have reached my ears. From this day forward all waters must seek only the lower levels. Rivers and streams will flow to greater rivers, to lakes, and to the seas. It will always be so."

Kwa'te then told Raven to fly quickly away to make the great magic which would cause the wishes of the great council to become fact within the world.

The preceding legend explains why Raven was held in the highest regard in the Puget Sound area of Washington State. Raven was considered the greatest of the supernatural creatures and was thought to possess great wisdom and powerful magic.

Raven legends, however, vary greatly among the different cultures of the coast natives. While the Puget Sound natives saw Raven as being wise and powerful, some Vancouver Island and British Columbian mainland tribes saw him in an entirely different light. To several tribes he was a thoughtless and inquisitive moocher, only a few degrees brighter than Blue Jay. Whatever his status, legends of Raven are numerous.

How Raven Lost his White Mantle
A Quillayute Version

During the early days of the Quillayute nation, the people fell on difficult times. Kwa'te, the Great Spirit, had given them land along Puget Sound in the forests near Hood Inlet. They built lodges there and prospered, enjoying their lives. The days were usually bright and warm during the summer months, which were long; and the winter rains kept the cold and the snow away.

In those days Kwa'te had entrusted to Grey Eagle power over water, fire, the sun, the moon, and the stars. Grey Eagle was supposed to keep the earth supplied with the proper amounts of sunlight and moonlight. He was supposed to supply adequate amounts of fire and water to the people. For a long time he did that.

Eventually, however, Grey Eagle grew vain and then he refused to share in equal proportions those things which Kwa'te had ordered him to share. Grey Eagle started to hoard the sunlight and in its place sent clouds filled with rain. The rain fell in excessive amounts on the land, but he kept the clouds there caring nothing for the plight of the Quillayute people.

While the Quillayute were miserable in their damp lodges, unable to hunt in the forest or venture onto the ocean to fish, Grey Eagle enjoyed the sunlight which he had locked up in his lodge high above the clouds.

After awhile the rain put out the fires in the villages, but Grey Eagle refused to listen to the pleas of the people. He ignored their songs of praise. Then Grey Eagle told the Quillayute there would be no more sunshine or moonlight as he was going to keep it all for his own use.

The Quillayute were greatly dismayed and appealed to Kwa'te for help. Kwa'te appeared to them, listened to their sad songs, and promised to help.

Kwa'te never intervened directly where his supernatural creatures were involved for that was not the way he had designed his world. Each of the lesser gods had a function and Great Spirit was reluctant to override their power, although he could have done so. He preferred to call on other gods who could persuade the offending one to relent. This method had always worked before and Kwa'te saw no reason why it would not prove successful again.

Kwa'te called on Raven, told him the story of the Quillayute peoples' plight and beseeched him to intercede with Grey Eagle on their behalf. Kwa'te felt that Raven would succeed because he was very wise and also friendly with Grey Eagle. Raven promised to help.

In those days, Raven was not a bird with black feathers. His feathers were pure white, befitting a god. He was dressed completely in a white mantle and even his beak and his feet were white for he was second only to Kwa'te, the greatest spirit.

Raven was truly majestic. His appearance commanded the greatest respect. There were other gods who wore the white mantle but none was completely white. Even Greatest Owl had feathers tipped with black and brown. Greatest Puffin had red and black among his white feathers. Raven was the only purely white god.

Raven was proud of his white mantle and he took great care to keep the dirt and grime from his feathers. He rarely stayed away from home for lengthy periods because his beautiful feathers always got dirty. Raven may have been very wise but, alas, he had grown very vain.

Raven gave much thought to his plan of action. He decided a quick move would be best so he would not be away from his home too long. As he walked slowly about his forest, his plan became clear in his mind. It was then he realized that he had walked to the edge of a clear lake. He stood for a long time on the shore admiring his reflection in the still water. He was so proud, his feathers so white, so beautiful that he decided then and there that he would do his task even more quickly than he had first decided. He wished to get home before his feathers became soiled.

Raven immediately took to flight and went directly to Grey Eagle's lodge. Grey Eagle welcomed him because he had not seen Raven for some time. He invited Raven to come inside the lodge which was warm and bright.

Once inside the lodge Raven very quickly discovered where Grey Eagle had hidden all the treasures. The minute Grey Eagle turned his back, Raven scooped up the sun, the moon, and the stars in his great talons. Then with his beak he grasped the clay pot which held the fire. He then flew quickly away, ignoring Grey Eagle's shouts imploring him to return his treasures.

Raven flew high into the sky where he scattered the stars about. Then he placed the sun in the middle of the sky and the moon he set away on the other side of the world opposite the sun. Then he began his return to the earth to give back the fire to the Quillayute people.

As Raven flew toward earth, the smoke from the fire blew back on him. Soon his beautiful white feathers were as black as night. The heat from the fire singed his beak until it, too, was black. The smoke irritated his eyes and they turned red. The heat from the coals singed his feet and they also turned black. The heat forced him to drop the pot and the fire fell to the earth.

Quillayute warriors gathered the fire and joyfully returned to their villages. Then they gathered and sang praises to Raven for he had delivered to them the sun and the moon and the stars and the fire. They did not know then of the trickery he had used. Had they known, their praises would have been less intense for the Quillayute warriors did not like such dishonorable deeds. But they would not learn of the deceit for a long time.

Raven returned home a dreadful sight. His entire body was as black as the darkest night. Try as he might he could not remove the soot. His feathers would not return to their former whiteness.

Raven appealed to Kwa'te. He begged the Great Spirit to change his feathers back to the white mantle. He pleaded with Kwa'te to change his feet and beak back to their former color.

"Oh, Raven," Kwa'te responded in sadness, "when I sought your help in this matter, I asked that you use your wisdom to convince Grey Eagle to return the treasures he was hoarding. Had you done so you would have gained the respect of all concerned. Instead, you acted with dishonor by taking advantage of Grey Eagle's hospitality to steal them. It is a crime against my laws to steal, as you well know."

"Oh Great Spirit," replied Raven, "I took such advantage in order not to be too long away from my home. I did not want to soil my feathers."

Kwa'te looked sadly upon his fallen child. A great sadness came into his eyes.

"Oh Raven," he said with sadness in his voice. "I am greatly distressed. To steal is bad enough, but you did so for reasons of vanity. Vanity is a sign of weakness and frailty of character. A god cannot be weak or show the traits of vanity. Because of this I can never return you to your former brilliance."

Raven wailed loudly. He chanted songs of remorse but Kwa'te remained unmoved. The Great Spirit left Raven in his despair. That is why ravens are pure black to this very day.

The Quillayute never forgot the great deed Raven had done for them. They were saddened that they could do nothing to help him regain his white feathers so they did the next best thing. They gave him the highest place possible on their lodge poles. The only time Raven is not on the top spot is when Thunderbird is included in the carving.

The Tse-Shaht tribe of Vancouver Island also have stories about Raven. Like the Quillayute they also know Raven had once been pure white. Unlike the Quillayute, the Tse-Shaht considered Raven as being a foolish, mooching pest.

Raven
A Tse-Shaht Story

One beautiful spring morning Raven was watching Kwi'kwa, the eagle, searching for salmon. Kwi'kwa soared high in the sky where he glided about for a long time watching for a plump salmon. Suddenly the eagle saw the one he wanted. He dived straight down to the surface of the ocean, extended his sharp talons, and plucked the salmon from the water in one graceful swoop. Raven marveled as he watched Kwi'kwa glide away to his home in the high trees in the forest.

Raven, who imitated others as a matter of course, decided he could also scoop salmon from the water just as easily as could the eagle. Raven flew from his perch in the tree and flew high into the sky. He drifted lazily on outstretched wings as he scanned the ocean far below. He was looking for a fat salmon.

Raven spotted several salmon, picked one as his target, then plummeted straight down just as he had seen the eagle dive. He headed downward directly at the salmon gathering speed as he fell.

Raven, however, was no fisherman. He had no real idea of the proper way to dive for salmon. He did not know that he had to dive at the place where the salmon would be by the time Raven reached the surface. Kwi'kwa knew the proper way and that is why he was nearly always successful when he went after salmon.

Raven also had gone into too steep a dive; he not only missed the salmon but he smacked into the water with such force that he was rendered unconscious. Raven would have surely drowned had not a passing sea otter seen him when he hit the water. The sea otter towed him back to shore and tugged him up onto the beach.

By the time Raven regained his senses the otter had already departed so he had no way of knowing how he had reached the shore. He decided he must have swam the distance and thought of what a mighty swimmer he was. Raven was embarrassed by his failure to catch a salmon but, as usual, he learned nothing from his misadventure and soon forgot. Once again Raven had failed to learn from his foolish behavior.

As Raven limped his way home he passed very close to a village where humans lived. He saw a group of women cooking salmon over a fire of hot coals. He stopped to watch and was amazed at how quickly the fish was cooked. The fish smelled delicious. Raven was overjoyed when one of the women tossed him a large morsel. Raven had never tasted cooked fish before and realized he had never eaten anything quite so good. He decided he would start cooking his fish instead of eating it raw.

Raven watched the women a while longer and decided he could easily learn to cook. He decided the best way to learn would be to watch one woman and learn her way. He selected a lodge and, for an entire day, he watched the woman who lived in it as she cooked. He watched closely as the woman cut the salmon into strips and placed them on the flat rocks which were resting on the hot coals. He noted how she poured oil from a clam shell over the fish as it cooked. Raven decided he could easily cook salmon. All he needed was a bed of hot coals, a large flat rock, and a clam shell.

Raven was not smart enough to practice by himself for a few days in order to learn all the proper procedures for cooking fish. He did not realize there was more to the art of cooking than what he had seen. Being very vain as well as being a terrible braggart, he felt he should impress the humans with his skills. He decided he would hold a great feast for the villagers to show them how well he could cook salmon.

He convinced himself that the humans would heap honors on him for his great talent and would carve totem poles of him and sing his praises during their ceremonial dances. Raven had always felt he should have a place high on the poles, even as high as Thunderbird, because he had such great talent, was so good at doing things, and because his feathers were as white as the snow on the top of the highest mountains.

Raven went down to the ocean and there he mooched a number of salmon from some sea otters who had caught a few too many and did not want to waste them. He took his salmon up to a clearing near the village then went about inviting all the villagers to his great salmon feast. The villagers agreed to come to his dinner that evening.

Raven's guests arrived at the appointed time expecting supper to be ready. Raven, however, had misjudged the time needed to heat the rocks and that caused a delay. Finally the rocks were hot enough and Raven placed his fish on them. Then he tipped his clam shell over the salmon expecting oil to pour from it. Of course, no oil poured out because Raven had not known the oil had to be put into the shell beforehand.

As he stood there trying to figure out why no oil was pouring from his shell the fish began to burn. He then realized he did not know how to turn the fish. He had not noticed how the woman had used a special piece of flat wood as a turner.

By now the smoke from the burning fish was so thick Raven was unable to see through it. As he stood there in the smoke wondering what he should do, his beautiful white feathers turned shiny black as did his beak. The heat from the rocks seared his tiny hands until they curled up to become claws.

Raven's guests, meantime, grew impatient. They knew there would be no great feast of salmon because the fish had all burned to ashes. One by one they all left for their own lodges muttering that of all the foolish things Raven had done over the years this was probably the most foolish.

Raven had now turned completely black from the sooty smoke. His eyes had been irritated by the smoke and were red from the heat.

The smoke had also affected his voice so he could no longer talk. All he could say was one word—a raucous kwa-kwa—and that one word is all he can say to this day. That is also what he is called by the Tse-Shaht people.

Why Nootka Totems
Place Crow above Raven
A Nootka Story

One sunny summer day when the world was young and birds and animals were the same as humans, Raven was walking alone on the outskirts of the village near the shore. He saw Mrs. Crow busily digging clams from the sand. He also saw that she had caught a small seal. He watched as she cut the seal into small pieces and placed these in a reed basket.

"Hello, my good woman," called Raven. "What is in the basket?"

"Clams," replied Mrs. Crow.

"There is something else as well," Raven stated. "May I have some?"

Mrs. Crow, knowing Raven was a mooch of the worst sort, ignored him. She hurried away to her home on the edge of the village. Once inside, she began to cook the seal and prepare the clams for supper.

Raven grew envious when he thought of the fine supper Crow would have when he returned home at the end of the day. He wondered how he could lay his hands on some of that supper for himself. Raven never worked for his own food. He preferred to mooch from others. He sat down on a rock to ponder the situation and was in midponder when a small boy approached.

"Hello, Raven," said the boy. "Will you play with me?"

"Of course," replied Raven. "What do you have in mind?"

"Oh, I don't know. What would you like to play?"

"Well," replied Raven, "in one good game I know, you run through the village shouting loudly that Beaver's lodge is on fire. Everyone will run to put out the fire and then we will laugh at them because they will look so funny running around in circles."

The boy thought that sounded like fun. He ran off yelling at the top of his voice that fire was burning down Beaver's lodge.

Just as Raven knew they would, the entire village cleared as all its inhabitants ran to the far end of the village where Beaver's house was located. Mrs. Crow joined the crowd, leaving her lodge unattended.

Raven rushed directly to Crow's house and went in. He took only a few minutes to eat all the clams. Then he started on the seal meat. The meat was so delicious that he ate and ate, forgetting about the time he was taking. As a result he stayed too long.

When the little boy had run through the village shouting about the fire he hollered so loudly that Youngest Crow, the son of Crow, heard him. Youngest Crow had, just that very minute, passed Beaver's house and, knowing there was no fire there, flew to the top of a tall tree to look around hoping to see where the fire really was. As he was looking he spied Raven entering his father's house. He wondered what was going on.

Youngest Crow flew as quickly as he could to where he knew his father was working. He told his father what he had seen. Crow flew as quickly as he could to his house. There he discovered Raven eating the seal which was to have been his supper.

Crow jumped on Raven's back and began pecking savagely at Raven's head. Raven hopped about frantically in his attempt to escape, but he could not break loose from Crow's grasp.

Finally, Crow tired of beating Raven and let him escape. By that time the entire village had gathered to watch Raven receive his well deserved thrashing.

Raven, humiliated and beaten, slunk from the village amid peals of laughter and hoots of derision. He remained hidden in the woods until darkness was well settled upon the world before he managed to work up enough courage to sneak back to the safety of his own house.

So that everyone would know for all time how Crow had bested Raven, the village artisan carved a totem pole. It showed Raven cowering in fear with Crow sitting atop him pecking at his head. As a result of that great fight so long ago, Nootka totem poles show Crow in a position higher than Raven.

According to Tsimshian lore, Ka'ah, the Raven, was once second only to Great Spirit in power and greatness. Raven, the greatest of all the supernatural creatures, had been trusted by all the animals as well as the humans. They all knew him as a benevolent god. Ka'ah had the ear of Great Spirit and was responsible for many good things which befell the Tsimshian people.

The Tsimshian also believed Ka'ah was responsible for Great Spirit's decision to deny immortality to humans. They did not, however, hold a grudge against him for the denial as they realized all things in nature were equal in the eyes of Great Spirit. It was, therefore, only right that only the gods should be immortal.

There are two versions of why immortality was denied the humans.

The Elderberry Bush and the Cliff
A Tsimshian Story

In the very early days, before the humans had been placed on the earth, Great Spirit and Ka'ah were together discussing the matter of the life span to be allotted to the humans. Great Spirit intended to place the humans on his earth, but could not decide if the humans should live forever. Ka'ah was uncertain also and suggested to Great Spirit to let the earth itself decide.

"How shall I do that?" asked Great Spirit.

Ka'ah pointed to a far away cliff. He then pointed to an elderberry bush that was growing at the base of the cliff.

"The spirit of the cliff and the spirit of the elderberry bush," Ka'ah said to Great Spirit, "are both pregnant. When the spirit of the elderberry gives forth her child it will be in the form of a flower, soft and fragile. It will live for a time and then will die. When the spirit of the cliff gives forth her child it will be in the form of a boulder, be hard and will live forever. Let the humans take the characteristics of the first child to come forth from their pregnant mothers."

"It will be so," agreed Great Spirit.

As time passed Ka'ah and Great Spirit watched closely, and as it happened both spirits gave birth within seconds of each other. But the Elderberry bush gave forth her child first so Great Spirit made his humans soft and mortal. But, because both births

103

had been so close, Great Spirit placed some of the rock in his humans so they would not be as fragile as the elderberry. The evidence of this are the finger and toe nails which adorn the human person and the spirit of endurance which is part of human character.

Wren Convinces Ka'ah
to Change his Mind
A Tsimshian Story

Ka'ah was with Great Spirit when the matter of human immortality was being discussed. Great Spirit was considering granting the right of eternal life to all his humans. Up to that point in time, death came to all eventually, but Great Spirit was beginning to think he might make changes.

As the two discussed the idea, Ka'ah agreed with Great Spirit. Before he could cast his final vote, however, a small wren who had been listening nearby flew to the ground before the two gods.

"If you grant immortality to the humans," the wren said, "I and my cousins will all perish. I beseech you to deny them that gift."

"Why, little one?" asked Raven. "How will such a gift deny you your life?"

"Oh, mighty Ka'ah," replied the wren. "Wrens build their nests in the burying boxes of dead humans. The tiny openings in the boxes are just the right size for our entrance, and the boxes are placed high enough that those who would harm us cannot reach."

Raven then argued that the wren should be afforded the protection he needed to safeguard his future, and Great Spirit agreed. Thus immortality was denied the humans.

Despite Raven's part in the denial of everlasting life the Tsimshian people sang his praises, carved his likeness on their lodge poles, and considered him a god for many years. That all changed following the days of the great flood after the water had receded and the humans returned to the lowlands to rebuild their lives.

Why Raven is Black
A Tsimshian Story

When the Tsimshian people returned to their valleys after the great flood they discovered that all the animals had disappeared. The also realized that the water had also disappeared leaving the rivers and the streams dry. There were no lakes or ponds. They knew the animals had survived the flood because, like the Tsimshian, the animals had gone into the hills where they had hidden until the water had receded. They knew the water was supposed to have returned to the same levels and amounts as before the flood because Great Spirit had promised them the world would return to the way it had been. The Indians called upon Ka'ah and asked him to find the animals and the water for them.

"Oh Great White Raven," they prayed, "find for us our fresh water and our animals. Rescue the water and the animals from the evil spirits who surely have them and hold them captive. Without the water we shall die of thirst, and without the animals those of us who do not die of starvation will surely perish in the freezing cold of the upcoming winter. We need the furs of the animals for clothing and the meat for food. Without the rivers and the lakes, we will be unable to catch the fish we need for food and for oil for our lamps."

Ka'ah, the Raven God, heard the prayers and with one mighty sweep of his huge wings took to the skies. In a moment he had crossed the highest peaks of the coastal range, passed over the Thompson and Okanagan valleys, moved along the length of the Kootenay Valley, and soared high above the Rocky Mountains. He swept across the lands furthest to the north and then went south across the great plains. To his dismay he could see neither animals nor water.

He turned back intending to search the western islands when his sharp vision caught a glint of light far to the north. In a trice he flew to where the sun had reflected the light. There he discovered the lights were tiny reflections from drops of fresh water dripping from the mouth of a huge toad.

This toad was monstrous in size and truly a loathsome being. Raven recognized him as an evil spirit and realized the toad had all the water stored inside his gigantic body. The spirit, convinced no one would ever find him, had fallen into a deep sleep. He did not see Raven in the sky.

Raven, calling on his great powers, crept up to the monstrous toad. Then, with a quick thrust of his huge beak, Raven punctured the toad's side. The water flowed out in a torrent and Raven gathered it all up in his great talons, rolled it into a tremendous ball, and flew away with it.

As Raven flew he let the water escape as a gentle rainfall. The rain fell to earth to the places where the lakes and rivers had been. Soon the lakes were full once again and the rivers and streams were flowing.

When the water returned, the fish, who had been sleeping in the mud, came out and began to swim around once more.

Ka'ah then flew to the highest peak of the highest mountain. There he pulled saplings from the ground and, returning once more to the valleys, planted the trees and shrubs so they could grow as they had before.

Having restored the water, the fish, and the trees, Ka'ah set out to find the animals. He flew very high and, when he was high enough to see the entire land, he scanned every inch of the ground below.

He searched high and low until at last he spied a large cabin hidden away in a remote valley. Using his great powers he looked through the cabin's roof and saw a little old lady sitting on a trap door which was in the middle of the cabin floor. Raven recognized the old crone as a very powerful evil spirit.

Raven then used more magic to look through the trap door. He could see all the missing animals in a deep pit below the cabin floor.

"Ah-ha," said Ka'ah to himself, "it will take all my magic to move the evil crone off that door. She is far too powerful for me to do that without using all my magic, and if I use all my magic moving her, I will have none left to open the trap door. I will have to trick her in some manner that will lure her away from the cabin."

He then sat down to think of a plan. He sat there for many days until, at last, a plan entered his mind. He flew quickly into the valley below where he changed to human form. In the disguise of a native hunter, Raven walked noisily to the cabin and knocked loudly on the front door.

"What do you want?" called the crone. "Why are you wandering about in my valley?"

"Hello, good woman," Raven called. "May I warm myself by your fire?"

"What do you want?" the crone called out again. "I do not want you in my valley. Go away at once."

But Raven pretended not to hear her. He opened the door a little crack and poked his head inside.

"Oh grandmother, I am but a poor hunter in search of some help. I have killed three elk from a large herd not far from here. I need a place to rest awhile before going to the next village to seek two or three good men who will help me carry my elk out of the woods."

"You lie!" the crone shrieked. "There can be no elk. I have all the animals. None are left to roam about."

"Grandmother," Raven replied, "An entire herd is in a ravine not far from here. I killed only three so there are many remaining."

"I don't believe you," the crone screamed. "You will show me this herd."

But Raven answered very casually that he was too tired and thirsty to lead her there, but that he would tell her where the herd was so she could go and see them for herself. He would stay in front of her fire until she returned. He knew she would never agree to that suggestion, but he knew that was what a hunter would suggest.

"Hah," the crone sputtered. "If I leave you here alone you will steal my possessions. You will take me to this herd. If you are lying to me, oh hunter, I will turn you into a rain dancer's hat."

"Very well," said Raven with obvious reluctance, "but you must then help me carry my elk from the forest. I will of course share the meat with you for your help."

The two then set off for the ravine. The old witch kept to the rear so she could keep an eye on the hunter.

They had gone some distance when Raven used his magic power to create a thick mist. The crone lost sight of him and he quickly changed himself into a squirrel and hurried through the trees until he came to the lodge.

He changed back into his proper form, and as Raven, he used all his great strength to force open the trap door. The animals all rushed out.

"Go quickly," Raven called to them. "Run as fast as you can and do not stop until you are far away. Run in all directions so the evil spirit will be unable to follow. Run! Run!"

Just as the last animal disappeared into the forest the old crone came rushing back toward the cabin.

"Stop! Stop at once," she cried. "You are all my pets. I am your mistress."

But none stopped and all, except Skunk, managed to escape. Skunk was in no hurry. She ambled along toward the deep woods stopping here and there to smell a flower or dig for a fat grubworm. Raven had urged her to run, but Skunk had ignored his shouts.

When the crone saw Skunk she ran to her and picked her up. But Skunk turned on the crone and bit her hand. The crone dropped Skunk who continued slowly on her way. The old crone was enraged. She waved her stick and called down a mighty curse upon Skunk.

"Go then," she screamed. "Go! But I will place on you an eternal curse. From this moment on—and for all time—you will give forth a terrible odor and neither human nor animal will ever be your friend again. All will avoid you forever, except Owl who will hunt you in the night. Owl will seize and eat you wherever he finds you."

That is the reason why skunks smell as they do, and why they are avoided by everyone except owls who remain the skunk's only natural enemy.

When the crone had finished putting her curse on poor Skunk she turned to Raven. She waved her stick at him and screamed dreadful threats. But Raven knew she could not harm him with her magic so he just stood there and laughed at her.

"I have defeated you, and I have released the animals you stole from the Tsimshian people," Raven told her. "You have no complaint."

"Ka'ah, oh mighty Raven," the old crone replied softly, "you may have defeated me, but it was not a fair contest. In a fair contest I might have bested you—what you did was deceitful. You used the crudest form of trickery and, above that, you lied. That is a great crime."

The crone then began to laugh at Raven. "I will defeat you yet, oh Raven. Hear me! I will petition Great Spirit and ask him to change your white feathers to black as punishment for your having broken the strictest of Great Spirit's laws. The loss of your white feathers will be my revenge. The black feathers you will then wear will be the evidence of the lie you told. Because of that no one—not even those you helped today—will ever trust you again."

At that she turned and walked away into the fog which still covered the land.

Raven knew she would have her revenge for he knew Great Spirit would have to punish him for his deceit. To break Great Spirit's law was the worst thing anyone could do. To tell the truth was the greatest of the laws. He knew he would lose the white mantle of a god.

However, Raven also knew he had saved the Tsimshian people by restoring the water and the animals, and that they would honor him for all time and remember his last great deed on their behalf. He knew he would always have a place of honor on the highest spot of their lodge poles which would adorn the villages for all time.

When the old crone took her complaint against Ka'ah to Great Spirit, there was no other decision which could be made.

Raven had lied in order to win a victory and to lie was a crime against the laws of Great Spirit. Raven was stripped of his white feathers.

Without the white mantle of a god, Raven became a lesser supernatural person and, although he still had considerable powers, he was no more powerful than any of the others. And, because he was no longer a god, he lost the adoration of the people and the animals just as the crone had prophesied.

The Tsimshian people still held him in the highest regard, but they no longer called on him as they once had. The animals, likewise, never called on him again. Only the birds, who were his cousins, and the fish, who had no reason not to trust him, remained his allies.

Raven called on the birds and the fish once in a while as several legends attest. One such legend tells of how Raven bested the rowdy spirit, Southwest Wind, with the help of his friends, the fish. It takes place long after Raven had lost his white feathers and shows how he was forced to rely more on intelligence and cunning than on the great magic he had once enjoyed.

How Raven Bested Southwest Wind
A Tsimshian Story

Southwest Wind had been blowing in the most boisterous manner for many days. He was causing all sorts of problems by blowing the roofs off the lodges and uprooting trees where the birds had their nests. The men of the villages were unable to go out in their canoes to fish. Everyone was upset and wished Southwest Wind would go away.

Raven was one of those who had grown annoyed. He could not understand why Southwest Wind was out and about because his season was supposed to be autumn and not summer. Raven called on him to stop. But, Southwest Wind just laughed at Raven and blew over the lodge pole in front of Raven's house. Raven, now thoroughly enraged, called his cousins, the birds, together.

"Cousins," Raven said to them, "Southwest Wind has become a nuisance and is causing far too many problems. He is blowing the berries off the bushes. If you don't fight back, you will soon have nothing to eat."

"We know that, oh Raven," they replied, "but what can we do?"

"If we all join together we can beat Southwest Wind with our wings. We will be too strong for him and he will be forced to quit."

Southwest Wind, however, had heard Raven. He knew Raven was right so he called his two sons and together they proved too much for the combined might of the birds. They had no choice but to give up the fight.

Raven then called on the animals, but they refused to help him as they thought he was trying to trick them for his own gain.

Finally, Raven walked down to the sea and called to the fish. He asked for their help and, though they were not being troubled by the wind, they agreed to help if they could. Raven had done the sea creatures a few kindnesses in the past and they decided they could repay him for his favors.

"How can we help, oh Raven?" Halibut asked. "We cannot leave the water and Southwest Wind will not come into the sea."

"I will use my magic to allow you to live for a time outside the water," promised Raven. "I will also make it possible for you to walk on the land while you are with me. I will return you all to the ocean in complete safety at the proper time."

The sea creatures agreed then to help. Raven chose Cod, Halibut, and Octopus as his warriors. Salmon and Mackerel, because they knew the vast reaches of the ocean, were selected to act as guides. Killer Whale allowed Raven to ride on his back for the journey to the home of Southwest Wind. That way, Killer Whale told Raven, he would be able to have all his strength when he arrived. The whale knew Raven would be tired from a long flight and his magic would be depleted as a result.

The tiny band set forth on the journey to the home of Southwest Wind. After four days and nights they came to a tiny island where the wind had his lodge. Southwest Wind had already returned to rest for a while before returning to the land for another assault. Raven flew quickly to the lodge and peered in through a window. He was pleased to see Southwest Wind sound asleep. He flew back to his tiny band and told them what he had seen.

"I have formed a good plan," he told them. "We will catch him as he sleeps and will force him to agree to our terms.

"Halibut, cover yourself with as many seaweeds as your body will allow. The extra seaweed will make you more slippery than usual. Then go and lie down in front of the lodge door.

"Cod, you will then sneak into the house and throw this red cedar bark on the fire. It will cause a great deal of smoke and Southwest Wind will awake with a fright. He will think his lodge is on fire and will run out as fast as he can. When he leaves his house he will step on Halibut's slippery body and will fall to the ground.

"When he falls, Octopus, you will grasp him firmly in all your eight great arms. Then you will drag him into the water. Allow only his head to remain above the surface. Then I will dictate to him the terms of his surrender."

All the fish agreed it was a good plan. They all took their places as Raven told them. Raven's plan went exactly as he had hoped it would. Cod threw enough bark on the fire to fill the house with smoke in only a few minutes, and when Southwest Wind came rushing out he slipped on Halibut's slimy body, fell directly into the clutches of Octopus, and before he realized what was happening to him, he found himself in the water with only his head showing above the surface.

"Southwest Wind," Ka'ah said to him, "you have behaved badly and have caused much trouble. You have violated the natural laws of the world by appearing out of your turn. As a supernatural creature I am justified in having Octopus pull you under the surface where you will drown."

"Oh mighty Ka'ah," pleaded the wind. "you have defeated me and I am at your mercy. I implore you to spare me. Do that and I will blow only gentle breezes which will be warm and mellow. And I will never appear again out of turn."

"I cannot agree to that," Raven answered. "Long days of warm wind will only dry the land. No one would benefit. I will spare you only if you agree to stay within your seasons, to blow only four or five days at a time then give way to the gentle Rain Spirit. Rain Spirit is a timid thing. She is afraid to come to the land while you are there."

"Oh Great Ka'ah," Southwest Wind said. "I hear your words and know you speak with great wisdom. I promise to do as you wish. I speak also for my sons who will heed their seasons as I will mine."

Southwest Wind's solemn promise was heard by all in the little band of warriors. They were bidden then by Raven to be the witnesses to the pact should Southwest Wind break his promise. They agreed to his request and Southwest Wind, knowing they would appear against him in council with Great Spirit should he break his word, vowed to remain faithful to his pact.

Then Octopus released the wind from his mighty grip. Southwest Wind scrambled ashore and fled into the forest highly embarrassed by the defeat. Since then, however, he has been as good as his word. That is the reason why there are always four or five days of warm winds followed by a day or two of gentle rain in the lands where Raven lives.

10 How Beaver Defeated Porcupine
A Chinook Story

On most totem poles of the interior villages, Beaver ranks higher than Porcupine. He is sometimes shown holding Porcupine down with a hand or a foot. This is because a Beaver once won a great victory over Porcupine.

In the early days of the world when the animals ruled the forests, Beaver and Porcupine got along quite well. Actually, they had very little to do with each other because Beaver was always busy building dams and had little time to socialize. Beaver had been charged by Tyee Sahale to form the river courses and lay out the ways the streams should run. This he did by damming up the waters until lakes had formed, then he would release the water so it would flow in the directions he had decreed it should. Beaver let out small amounts of water for small rivers like the Okanagan River, which is very small and very short, and he would let out vast amounts of water for great rivers like Columbia and Skeena. In this way, he started rivers of all sizes and importance.

Porcupine, on the other hand, had been given no tasks by Great Spirit. For some reason he had been overlooked when Tyee Sahale designated the work. Instead of asking for something to do, Porcupine stayed silent and lived a life of ease. He did nothing at all except wander aimlessly through the forests going from one tree to another eating tender leaves during the fine weather, and eating bark during the winter weather.

When times became truly hard he ate anything he could, including the posts which held up his neighbors' houses. Even to this day his descendants will gnaw at ax handles and the floor boards of cottages when they get hungry during the cold winter months. This is because the first Porcupine, unlike the first Beaver, never learned how to work or to store food for the winter months. For the first Porcupine life was too easy and he thought the good times would never end. He saw no reason to put aside food as did the other animals.

Everything did go well during the first few years. But one year there came to the forests a very evil spirit who created many bugs. The evil spirit told the bugs to get into all the poplar trees and eat all the leaves. The bugs ate all the leaves and this caused the trees to fall ill. The bark fell off the trees and soon there was nothing for Porcupine to eat. He began to worry.

As luck would have it, Porcupine came across a supply of trees which Beaver had cut down for his own use during the winter. These trees were still healthy and had nice green leaves. Porcupine, thinking he would not be seen, stole all the leaves and was slinking away with them when Beaver returned.

Beaver called to Porcupine to return the leaves. Porcupine refused. He insisted that because he and Beaver were related, regardless of how distant the relationship was, they must share with each other. He made no mention of the fact that he had never shared anything with Beaver.

Beaver would have none of that. He moved closer, intending to clout Porcupine with his flat tail. But Porcupine struck first. He lashed out with his tail and all Beaver got for his troubles was a nose full of quills. He fled to his village in great pain.

Beaver had friends who helped him take the quills out of his nose. Then they formed a raiding party, journeyed to Porcupine's village, and captured him. They carried him in a canoe to an island in the middle of a nearby lake where they left him.

The island had only a few trees on it and none of them were edible. Porcupine feared he would starve to death because the trees were no good to him as food and he could not swim away from the island. He began to wail—loudly in a most tormented voice—a song of praise to his friend North Wind.

"Oh, great North Wind I do beseech thee, make the cold weather come. Cause the lake to freeze that I may return safely to my lodge."

North Wind heard the songs of praise and beseeching. He responded by sending blasts of cold wind which froze the lake.

Porcupine scurried across the ice to the safety of his own village. Once home, he told his neighbors what had happened. They decided to avenge the humiliation.

Porcupine's friends went silently to Beaver's lodge where they found him sound asleep. Before he could awaken and call out, they grabbed him and carried him away into the forest. Finding a tall tree, they carried him all the way to the top and left him there, stranded.

Beaver, of course, was unable to climb trees. He was no more able to climb down than he was to climb up. He sat alone on the highest branch in silent despair. Beaver had no idea of what he could do. He tried calling out, but he was so high his voice was drowned out by the wind. He knew he was on his own. He feared he would starve to death for he knew he could not survive for long at the top of a tree.

Suddenly, he knew what he could do. He was surprised he had not thought of it sooner. He began to gnaw away at the tree. He gnawed the tree away foot by foot until it was only a couple of feet high. Then he jumped down, returned home, and told his neighbors what had happened.

The entire village went to Porcupine's home, and when Porcupine saw Beaver standing before him unharmed, he was very surprised. He asked Beaver how he had managed to escape from the tall tree. When Beaver told him the story, Porcupine admitted Beaver was smarter than he. The shamans of the villages declared that Beaver had indeed defeated Porcupine because he had escaped from his predicament through his own resources whereas Porcupine had sought help from North Wind in order to escape his exile.

All of the creatures agreed that Beaver was the smarter of the two. From that day forward when totem poles were carved they always showed Beaver in a higher position than Porcupine.

But Beaver never forgot the pain he had suffered from the quills Porcupine had jabbed into his nose. He decided he would never again speak to Porcupine. So, in one way at least, Porcupine had bested Beaver because, to this day, you will never see a beaver go anywhere near a porcupine, even if the porcupine is eating the leaves off the tree the beaver has just brought down.

11 Beyond the Sacred Pool

The natives who inhabited the West Coast, similar to their prairie and eastern contemporaries, saw life and all things in the world as part of nature. Everything had been created by Great Spirit and these creations were assisted along the way by lesser spirits doing the bidding of the Great Spirit.

Indians believed that all things—trees, bushes, winds, rain, rocks, animals and humans, fire, water, day and night, flowers, birds, and insects—had unique individual spirits, the energy of life itself. Because these things all had a spirit, they were able to speak with the greater spirits in their own individual languages. Each had its own voice, its own songs, and its own prayers. The natives gathered their inspiration from all of nature.

The winds blowing from the different directions carried voices of beings from far away. To each wind separate names were given. The wind spirits influenced the seasons and controlled the weather. Therefore the wind spirits were sacred and were honored or feared as befitted their status. In none of the various Indian languages can the words for *sacred* be defined as necessarily meaning *good* as they can be in most religions.

Whether the sacred spirit was good or evil depended entirely on the way it helped or hindered the Indian in his everyday life. A raging blizzard was certainly no help so it was considered as having the spirit of an evil deity. On the other hand, a gentle rain helped the growth of berries and grains and was therefore possessed of a good spirit.

Whether the spirits were good or evil, they were all held to be sacred and beyond the understanding of humans. Because the spirits were so powerful and could aid or destroy the work of humans, it was always in everyone's best interests to curry favor with them if only to escape the wrath of the evil ones.

Water spirits were sometimes evil and could be neither seen nor heard. That explained why a swimmer could disappear without a trace or a canoe could suddenly overturn without warning. There were, of course, good water spirits who supplied fish and other benefits such as the medicinal qualities of certain seaweeds.

Spirits of swamps and dense forests were always evil, could be heard but never seen, and were to be avoided by staying out of their domains. The forest and swamp spirits usually slept during the day to restore the energy they expended during the night when they prowled about grabbing travelers who had been foolish enough to venture out in the darkness. Disobedient children were told to mend their ways lest they be taken by the forest demons.

To many of the tribes the Storm Spirit was Thunderbird, the most powerful of all the supernatural creatures. The great Thunderbird, serving as Great Spirit's messenger, delivered messages to the shamans through the medium of thunderclaps and lightening flashes.

Most tribes feared Thunderbird above all other spirits whether good or evil. None considered him to be evil but few thought he was good either. Of all the spirits, Thunderbird alone had no precise definition. His volatile disposition seems to have ruled the different opinions. If he was in a good frame of mind he was good; if he was cranky or displeased he could become very evil indeed.

Thunderbird produced storms by flying across the skies high above the clouds which he had gathered to hide his flight. The flapping of his huge wings caused thunder while the light he flashed from his eyes caused the lightening which lit his way.

All the storytellers had Thunderbird residing in a cave at the top of the highest mountain in the world, usually the highest one visible in the tribe's particular territory. No Indian would ever consider angering this spirit by encroaching upon his mountain, even those from tribes which considered him a benevolent spirit. The Haida did not particularly fear this spirit, but the Nootka and the Kwakiutl did.

Some spirits had far more magic than others. Some had powers limited to night or day, winter or summer. Many, like North Wind, slept during the summer months.

Many spirits were not spirits in the strictest sense of the word. These were the supernatural people and the supernatural animals. Itopolos, the Coyote God of the Waso tribe of northern California, was a supernatural animal, leader of all supernaturals and second only to the Great Spirit. Unlike most of the supernaturals, Itopolos could not only be heard, he could also be seen.

Supernatural people could assume animal or bird form, could become rocks or trees, or take on human shape as they pleased. However, whatever shape they assumed, they remained pale and ghostlike and were thus easily identified. They appeared rarely, and when they did it was solely to guide the Indians through troubled or dangerous times.

Supernatural people were not gods, for they had once been human. Through some great deed or by leading an exemplary life or displaying some tremendous talent in art or craftsmanship, a human could be rewarded by Great Spirit. There was no higher reward than being made a supernatural person.

The Haida put great faith in supernatural people. Their belief in these magical entities seems to have been far more extensive than that of other coastal tribes. This is understandable, considering that Haida lands were mainly along the northern coast.

Haida-Gwai, to give the Haida land its true name, is enshrouded for much of the year by mists. The rainfall in that part of the country is above average. While snow is not excessive, winters are usually cold and damp. The small islands north of the Queen Charlotte group are usually foggy and mist enshrouded while the dense forests are always dark and foreboding. To the naturist mind of the first Haida people such an area had to be a magic place ideally

119

suited for ghostly beings. It is no wonder the Haida believed these misty lands were home to spirits and ghosts. It is even smaller wonder that travel to these islands was very rare.

The Haida recognized many supernatural people. Most were of minor importance, figuring little in the stories and legends of the early days. The most important numbered thirteen, and of these, Fair Weather Woman and Master Carpenter, the earthly parents of Tsin, the Sun God, were listed near the top in importance. But what of the other eleven? These are the ones who are the most difficult to interpret. Their original function in the scheme of things has not to date been fully explained. Many theories have been put forward, some of which make a good case, but others hold little substance. The Haida people themselves appear at odds with each other over the meaning of the tales concerning these mysterious eleven. Modern Haidas are generally of two minds and the debate will likely rage for years to come. It is not the intent of this book to enter the debate. It will suffice to simply tell the story told to me many years ago by a Haida shaman.

The Tale of the Ten Brothers
A Haida Story

There were once ten brothers who journeyed to the misty islands where Fair Weather Woman and Master Carpenter live. While there, the brothers decided to climb a high mountain, but as they neared the top a sudden mist enveloped them. They could neither climb down nor proceed higher. Realizing they were stranded, they decided to light a fire and spend the time waiting for the mist to clear.

As they huddled about the fire the youngest brother idly tossed an arrow into the flames and watched it burn. The arrow was totally consumed in strangely bright flame. Then, suddenly, the mist parted enough for the brothers to see the arrow lying on the ground below. Puzzled, the youngest brother then tossed his bow into the fire. The bow was immediately consumed by a bright flame. Once again the mist parted to reveal the intact bow on the ground beside the arrow.

Certain that this was a sign from Great Spirit, the younger brother stepped into the fire. He was immediately consumed by the flames. Seconds later the mist parted to reveal him standing on the ground holding the bow and the arrow. He beckoned to the others to follow his example.

After some hesitation, the remaining nine brothers entered the fire one by one where the flames consumed them. They were each in turn reunited on the ground below. They were puzzled by the change in their appearance and asked each other about it. None had any answer. Although they were still of human form, they were now the consistency of smoke and their eyes were bigger. Aside from that they were the same as before.

Following some discussion they decided to reenter their canoe and return to their village. Soon they were paddling briskly through the choppy waters toward home. They had paddled many hours when they spied a village a short distance ahead. They swung their canoe toward the shore and approached the village.

As the canoe neared the beach the brothers heard a shaman calling loudly to the villagers, "Behold! The supernatural people approach."

The brothers, confused by the calling, turned and paddled back to the deeper waters.

Some time later they approached a second village. This time, as the canoe touched ashore, the youngest brother stepped out and stood on the beach.

As he stood there a shaman approached carrying a basket of food which he gave to the brother. Then he called out to the villagers in a loud voice, "Behold! He Who Casts the Bow steps ashore."

The brothers then paddled on until they came to a third village. Once again they brought their canoe to the beach. This time the second youngest brother stepped out of the canoe. As at the previous village, a shaman approached carrying a basket of gifts for the brothers. He called out to the villagers, "Behold! He Who Has the Hawk Heart steps ashore." After accepting the basket, the brothers once again departed and continued their travels.

Their journey continued with the same results at each village they visited. Every time the brothers, each in his turn, went ashore, they were greeted by a shaman who presented a basket of gifts. At each village, as the brother accepted the basket, the shaman would call to the villagers the brother's supernatural identity.

At the fourth village the shaman called, "Behold! He on Whom the Daylight Rests steps ashore."

At the fifth village the shaman called, "Behold! He on Whom the Sunshine Lights the Water steps ashore."

At the sixth village the shaman called, "Behold! He Who Is a Puffin on the Water steps ashore."

At the seventh village the shaman called, "Behold! He Who Is a Hawk Rising From the Water steps ashore."

At the eighth village the shaman called, "Behold! He Who Wears Clouds About His Neck steps ashore."

At the ninth village the shaman called, "Behold! He Who Has the Big Eyes steps ashore."

At the tenth village the shaman called, "Behold! He Who Guides from the Back of the Canoe steps ashore."

At the eleventh village as the eldest brother stepped ashore, he was greeted by the shaman in a most reverent manner. The shaman offered a gift of many fine fish which the eldest brother accepted. Then the shaman called out to the villagers, "Behold! He Who Speaks Partly in the Words of the Raven steps ashore."

It was at this point that the brothers realized they had, by stepping into the fire, obeyed a sign from Great Spirit and that they were supernatural people. They understood now why they had the appearance of smoke. They also realized that others saw them differently than they appeared to each other. Still, they did not understand the reasons why they had been chosen or what functions they were expected to perform.

Continuing their journey the ten brothers visited a twelfth village where once again they were offered a basket of gifts. When they accepted the gifts, they were brought a woman who had been badly burned by a fire. The shaman asked the brothers to cure her burns.

The brothers took the woman to their canoe and told her to lie down in the bottom. Then the eldest brother took his knife and cut a small hole in the bottom of the boat.

"Woman," he ordered, "bathe yourself in the water that enters the canoe through the hole in the floor."

She did as she was told and her burns healed at once. She was told she could then return to her village, but she begged to be allowed to remain. She told the brothers she wished to remain with them as she had been told in a dream to say this to them. She told them that she was to earn her keep by bailing the water which would enter the canoe. She was then told she could stay.

The brothers knew they would be unable to return to their original village, but they were unsure of what to do. They paddled out to sea hoping to see a sign which would tell them where they should go. They paddled toward the north for awhile, then turned west, then south, then east. No sign was forthcoming so they turned once again on a northward course.

They were on their second swing to the north when a gull appeared and gave a sign that it should be followed. The brothers did so and the gull led them to a place called Dju on the northern tip of the biggest island. There they were met by Fair Weather Woman who called to them by the names each had been given by the various shamans. She also greeted the woman and told her she would be a supernatural person known as Woman Who Bails the Canoe. She would guard fishermen who became lost on the sea.

Pointing to an island barely visible on the horizon, Fair Weather Woman told the eleven travelers to proceed there at once.

"Go there and a wizard will paint you as he will paint all others who become supernatural people. When you are painted you will put on the clothing he will give you. You will then dance four nights at the end of which you shall enter the misty land."

They went at once to the island where the wizard painted them each in the manner befitting their individual positions in the hierarchy of the supernatural people. Then he dressed them in the clothing of their positions and watched as they danced for four nights. When the dancing had ended the wizard enshrouded their canoe in a cloud whereupon they departed for the misty land.

Thus the eleven became supernatural people. These are the ones who speak through the shamans, delivering the messages which Great Spirit wishes to give to the Haida people from time to time.

The interesting aspects of the Indians' beliefs in supernatural people, supernatural creatures, and various supernatural animals are the coincidental patterns which can be compared to other societies and religions most of which are far removed in time and locale.

Tsin, Sky God of the Haida people, came among his people as a tiny baby and lived with them for about thirty summers. He had chosen as his mother a maiden in her teens, unwed and as yet unbetrothed. He chose as his father a gifted carpenter. When he left his earthly status, he bestowed on his parents the status of immortality as supernatural people.

His parents were notified of their important tasks by supernatural creatures, the maiden by Greatest Eagle and the carpenter by Greatest Sea Otter. The finding of the baby in a cockleshell may be compared to Pharaoh's daughter finding Moses in a basket of reeds in the ebbing tide.

If the early missionaries noticed the similarities in the Haida tale of Tsin and the story they were expecting the Haida to accept, they either refused to acknowledge the similarities or they simply did not listen to the Haida version. It is suspected the latter is the case.

All the tribes held beliefs in some sort of afterlife, but not a single one gave any consideration to eternal punishment in some defined place of torment. The afterlife, to the Indian, involved the spirit undertaking a long journey to the Land of Ghosts or to the Land of Mists where the spirit would undergo a transformation to some sort of supernatural human.

Only those who had lived lives of honor, respect, and trustworthiness could expect the rewards of an untroubled afterlife. Those who lived outside the bounds of a righteous life would be refused entry to the sacred places. This meant their spirits must roam aimlessly for eternity never knowing any rest. There is no mention in Indian legend, not even in oblique terms, of any place remotely resembling the hell that the missionaries eventually told them about.

The various Indian societies had differing versions of the afterlife, but most varied only slightly. All agreed that the spirit, once released from its mortal shell, undertook a long journey to the spirit world. The journey varied mainly in the means used for transportation which encompassed every means of travel known to the Indians. Some journeyed across a vast ocean in a canoe. One inland band envisioned a long bridge over which the spirit walked for many months before arriving at an ultimate destination.

Most of the coast tribes subscribed to the canoe journey. They believed the departed spirit boarded a supernatural canoe which he paddled to the Land of Mists. There he was met by a supernatural person. If the deceased had led a good life, he was welcomed and taken to the wizard who painted him according to his new status, gave him robes of brightly colored cloth, and sent him into the misty land of souls.

On the other hand, if the deceased was rejected because of having led an evil life, he would be placed back into his canoe, cast adrift, and left to paddle aimlessly for all eternity knowing no rest and denied any landfall.

Some inland tribes believed the soul traveled many days along a lonely path until it came to a pool of fresh, cool water. It would drink of this water whereupon it would shrink to a size small enough to allow entry through a very narrow crevice in the sky. The crevice of course was the entrance to the Land of Ghosts.

Once inside the other world, the soul would be met by the Keepers, the guardians of the Land of Ghosts. The Keepers would offer the soul spiritual food. If the soul had led a good life the food would be accepted, but the soul could not swallow the food if its human life had been less than righteous, for the food would not stay in the mouth.

If the food was rejected, the Keepers expelled the soul from the Land of Ghosts. Once cast out the soul would never again be able to find the sacred pool and would, therefore, be unable to try again for entry. From then onward, the soul, having returned to full size, was doomed to roam about the earth forever. Invisible, without substance, friendless, and alone, it became a Homeless One.

The Chinook people believed each human had two souls—Great Soul and Lesser Soul. During serious illness, comas, or periods of unconsciousness Lesser Soul would be called by the Keepers. Lesser Soul would speed to the Land of Ghosts where it would be detained while the Keepers debated whether or not the human below had fulfilled his mission on earth. The debate could last a few seconds or many months, for the Keepers had no limit on their time.

If the Keepers decided to extend the life of the stricken human, they would release Lesser Soul and send it back with magic they had supplied. Lesser Soul would work the magic which would break the coma and drive away the evil sickness.

If the Keepers decided the human's life should end they would call out to Great Soul. Great Soul would then depart its human body and begin the long walk along the sacred path to the sacred pool from whence it would either enter the Land of Ghosts for all time or become a Homeless One according to the record of his life on earth.

12 Why There is Never Harm in Listening

A Cowichan Story

Canoes were invented during the very early days but, as would be expected, the first ones were not of good quality. The first canoe was only a big tree which had been cut down and hollowed out with fire and crude axes. It was very difficult to handle, was hard to steer, and, as paddles had not been invented, was hard to move through the water. They carried very few people, but by using these crude boats, the Indians managed to move farther afield than they would have had they remained afoot. The use of such boats expanded their horizons and encouraged trade with neighboring tribes.

Before long, certain men saw the advantages of water travel and began to think about making wooden canoes which would be lighter, hold more men, and glide easily through the water. These men were carpenters who were already adept at building houses out of planks which they cut from the great trees which grew all around them. They began to imagine how they might use planks of wood to build boats. They had already invented paddles and before long they discovered the art of boat building.

Those first boats, while seaworthy and acceptable, had many faults. They leaked, required continuous bailing, and often broke up in heavy seas. Sometimes they capsized for no apparent reason.

The carpenters persisted and over the years they improved the boats by learning how to wedge the wooden planks so they would hold tightly to the frames. Then someone discovered that by mixing special oils with the resin from certain trees, they could produce a sticky substance that would seal the planks and keep the sea water out.

Still, the boats lacked strength in rough water. This failing seemed insurmountable for many years. Even the best carpenters felt there was no solution to the question. The men who used the boats, fishermen and hunters mostly, had to limit their travels to days when the sea was calm; but the population of the villages was increasing so the need for fish and meat became greater.

The carpenters continued to work hard trying to solve the problem, but none was able to perfect the great wooden canoes. Though the boats were stronger than ever, they could not withstand the rough seas in which they were required to travel.

Then one day the best carpenter of the time, a Cowichan who lived on the east coast of Vancouver Island on an inlet called Nanoose, was working on a new canoe. He was suddenly aware that he was being watched and looked up to see a pale, ghostly figure standing near a tree. The Indian stopped his work and turned to face the stranger. He realized his visitor was a supernatural person, for he had once seen such people while on a journey to the misty lands to the north.

"I greet you most humbly, oh supernatural person," he said to his visitor. "May I welcome you to my lowly place of work?"

The ghostly one did not reply, but motioned that the carpenter should carry on with his work. The carpenter, realizing his visitor intended only to watch, returned to his labors.

After a time the supernatural person spoke, "I, oh carpenter, am called Greatest Fool, the supernatural person who attends to the affairs of mortal idiots by watching over them so they will come to no harm."

"It is indeed said that a good spirit watches over and protects idiots and fools," the carpenter answered. "I have heard that said many times and I know it to be true."

"It is also said," continued Greatest Fool, "that those who are considered imbeciles are thought to be hopelessly stupid. Is that not a common belief?"

"There are those who consider that to be true," replied the carpenter, speaking very cautiously. To offend a supernatural person could have grave consequences.

"Would you," asked Greatest Fool, "listen to the opinion of an imbecile?"

The carpenter hesitated not a moment before answering, "I would even listen to the squawkings of foolish Blue Jay if he could tell me why my great canoes cannot withstand the roughness of the ocean. I would not only be pleased to hear such a person, I would carve a tall pole in his honor."

Greatest Fool nodded but did not reply. Suddenly he was gone. The carpenter returned to his work. He began to think that perhaps he had only imagined his visitor. After a few days had passed he forgot about the visit.

Many days passed. The carpenter had almost finished his canoe, and was about to place the wedges into their proper positions, when he once again realized he was being watched. Turning, he saw a boy whom he knew to be the youngest son of a fisherman. The boy had been born in great difficulty, which had left him with an addled mind. Though the boy had grown as would any normal boy, he could barely speak and had been unable to learn anything but the most menial of tasks. He spent his time helping the women wash clothes, and sometimes they let him cut the meat and fish before it was placed on the smoke racks.

Occasionally the boy watched the carpenter at his work, but he had rarely said anything. The carpenter had always been kind to the boy and had never told him to leave, even if he got in the way. The carpenter believed, as did all coastal people, that he must treat such people with kindness.

After watching for a few minutes, the boy spoke in his halting manner, "Will this boat be good?"

The carpenter stopped his work. He turned to the boy and smiled sadly. "I do not know," he said softly. "I have built it better than the others. I have increased the size of the wedges, and I have sealed it with a thicker sealant. Yet, I very much doubt that it will prove to be better than the others."

He didn't think his words meant much to the boy. He held a wedge out to him and explained how they worked.

"The wedges you use are always straight?" asked the boy.

"Yes. Straight wedges bind tightly," the carpenter replied. "But they always work loose. Then they give way."

"Maybe you should use wedges that are curved," the boy said. Then, having lost interest, he wandered off into the woods to look for butterflies.

It was then that the carpenter remembered the words of Greatest Fool. He wondered if the supernatural person had been testing him. He decided to give the boy's idea a try. He had nothing to lose.

The carpenter took his wedges and began to cut them into curved shapes. He worked carefully so they would fit snugly into place. When the boat was finished he called his sons who helped him put it into the water. The next morning they went out into the deep water where the waves were high. Even the waves made by the southeast wind could not harm the boat. It held firmly together, did not leak, and moved more easily through the water than had any of the others built to that time.

This is how the custom of using curved wedges began. The carpenter, remembering his promise to Greatest Fool, carved a totem pole to honor the idiot boy who had spoken so wisely. By carving the pole, the carpenter reminded the people that even those who appear to be fools are often capable of producing good ideas from time to time.

As the carpenter learned, it never hurts to listen.

13 Why the Deer and the Wolves are Enemies

A Siwash Story

In the ancient days when the world was very new and Tyee Sahale had not yet caused humans to be on the land, the animals held dominance over the earth. They were magical creatures who could walk upright if they chose to, could speak, and had many human qualities. Tyee Sahale watched over them protecting them from the evil spirits which roamed the lands, but he never interfered in their daily lives. This he would not do for he wanted them to find their own solutions to everyday problems.

The Deer people lived in the deep forest. They were fleet of foot and lived on grass and the delectable leaves of trees. The Deer people did not hunt or fish as meat was not to their liking. They had dealings with all of the other animals except the Wolf people and the Cougar people as the Wolves and the Cougars were their enemies. The Deer were faster than the Wolves and Cougars, but they feared them because those who were caught were either taken as slaves or eaten. The Deer's only defense was to run as they did not own weapons and were unable to fight.

During the warm weather, the Deer people moved about the forest gathering food for the winter months. They traveled in pairs or in small groups and were always alert to the presence of their enemies. The Deer people liked the summer because they were always warm. In winter their lives became difficult.

During the winter the rains came and often the snow as well. When the snow covered the ground the Deer people became very cold so they spent the long months huddled together in sheltered areas of the forest, trying to stay warm as best they could. They wondered what they could do to help keep themselves warm. One cold winter they called out to Tyee Sahale. They sang songs of praise and asked for warm weather to be sent.

Tyee Sahale was never willing to change his system to accommodate any single group. He sent Thunderbird to deliver his reply to the Deer peoples' prayers.

"Tyee Sahale," roared Thunderbird, "will send neither South Wind nor the warm weather spirit to this part of the earth because they are busy elsewhere. If you wish to warm yourselves you should capture a cousin of the fire spirit and build a campfire to sit around. Then you will all be warm."

"We have only heard of the fire spirit," Deer Chief replied. "We do not know where to find one."

"The Wolf people have fire," Thunderbird advised. "Get some from them. You will have to figure out how to get it, though, as they will never give it up willingly."

"Can you tell us how to go about getting a fire spirit from the Wolf people?" Deer Chief begged. He was not at all anxious to have dealings with the Wolves.

"Tyee Sahale gave the Deer people nimble feet with which to run," Thunderbird growled. "I assume he also gave them nimble brains with which to think. I have given you the answer. It is up to you to figure it out. Now, you must excuse me. I must be away. I do not like staying in the forest. It is too cold and too damp." With a parting roar he rose into the sky, spread his huge wings, and flew off to his cave in a high mountain far to the north.

After Thunderbird had left, the Deer people held a conference. The only topic was the question of how to get the Wolf people to give up one of the fire spirits. No one had any answer however, and it never occurred to any of them to ask a friendly tribe to spare one of theirs. Other people had fire, but Thunderbird had only mentioned the wolves so the Deer thought that was the only group who had fire.

The discussion went on for many hours, but there was no decision made as the Deer all knew the wolves would demand too high a price for a fire spirit. Wolf Chief would demand many Deer people be sent to his village to become slaves—or worse.

Deer Chief found himself alone with the problem. Because he was the chief he was expected to come up with the answer. For many days and nights he sat alone, shivering in the cold, pondering ways which might bring a fire spirit to his people.

Suddenly, he had an idea. He knew the Wolves were fond of dancing. He had watched them from the safety of the woods as they danced around their fires. He had admired the way the dancers stepped, but he knew the Deer were better dancers. And that, he decided, was how he would get the fire spirit. He realized the Thunderbird's mention of nimble feet was the message from Tyee Sahale.

Once he had given his plan some deep thought, he felt sure it would work. The next morning he set off for the village of the Wolf people. He had gone only a short distance when he was stopped by a Hawk who appeared suddenly with a message from Tyee Sahale.

"I am to accompany you on your journey, oh Chief of the Deer people," the Hawk said. "Tyee Sahale has told me to act as your messenger, and also to watch as you carry out your plan so I may warn you if the Wolf people plot treachery against you while you are in their village."

"Does Tyee Sahale know what I plan to do?" asked Deer Chief.

"Of course," replied the Hawk. "Tyee Sahale knows all things. He will not help you, though, once you begin. From start to finish you must do all things on your own initiative. If you succeed you will entice a fire spirit, but if you fail...." The Hawk did not finish the sentence, for Deer Chief knew the answer well enough.

The two set out again on the trail to the Wolves' camp, with the Hawk flying high overhead scouting the way. He would warn Deer Chief when Wolves were nearby and the Deer would hide until they had passed. Then he would return to the trail.

After many hours Deer Chief came within sight of the Wolves' village. He decided to wait for dawn as it would be unwise to approach the village at night. The Hawk agreed and settled into a tree where he could watch from a safe distance.

When morning arrived, Deer Chief signaled the Hawk to come to his side. Deer Chief asked him what he had seen in the Wolves' village. The Hawk replied that everything seemed to be normal. A fire was burning in the center of the village, and the Wolves were busy at their work. He said he had also seen several Deer slaves in the village.

"Oh Hawk, my brother," said Deer Chief, "go to the village of the Wolves. Tell Wolf Chief that I have seen his people as they danced about their fire. Tell him I have admired the way they dance and that I would like to dance with them. Tell Wolf Chief that I wish to perform for him the dance of the Deer people."

"Wolf Chief will wish to know why you want to do all this for him," the Hawk stated.

"Indeed he will," Deer Chief answered. "When he asks tell him only that all will be revealed to him the moment my dance ends."

The Hawk then flew off to the village of the Wolves. He met with the chief and told him all Deer Chief had said. The Wolf, as expected, was puzzled why a Deer would want to dance for him, but the Hawk told him only that he would know the answer when the dance ended. Wolf Chief then agreed to meet with Deer Chief. He promised safe passage into the camp.

When the Hawk returned to Deer Chief's hiding place, he told him the details of his meeting with Wolf Chief. He also warned him the Wolf was planning treachery as he only promised safe passage to the village, but had said nothing about leaving with the same guarantee.

"I," said the Hawk, "am a supernatural creature as you know. I know what you plan to do, but I am curious how you plan to entice a fire spirit from the wolves' fire."

"Oh great Hawk," Deer Chief replied, "I have tied leather thongs to my legs. I will dance close to the fire and while so doing will sing songs of praise to the fire spirits. The wolves will not understand the words of my song because I will sing in the language of the Deer. If the fire spirits are willing, one or two will attach themselves to the thongs and I will carry them to my village."

"I see," said the Hawk. "I wish you great success."

"There is something I would ask of you, oh Hawk," Deer Chief said. "I have a plan which will free the slaves who are now captive in the village. Will you help me in that endeavor?"

"Tell me what you would have me do, oh chief," the Hawk replied, "and I will help however I can."

Deer Chief quickly outlined his plan and the Hawk agreed to help. Then Deer Chief moved quickly through the forest until he came to the edge of the wolves' village. Wolf Chief came to meet him. Deer Chief saw the Hawk fly to a perch in a nearby tree and he felt safer. He knew Wolf Chief would honor his promise for safe conduct so long as the Hawk was watching.

"Welcome, oh Chief of the Deer people," Wolf Chief called in greeting. "We are pleased that you wish to dance with us. We are also curious and wish to know your reasons."

"I wish to dance with your people in hopes of bettering our relationship with each other," Deer Chief said, rather vaguely.

"How can there be friendship between your people and mine?" asked Wolf Chief. "Your people are our main source of food and slaves. Friendship between our people would deny the wolves that source. We would not survive long without the Deer."

"I am fully aware of that," replied Deer Chief, "but I am fully prepared to enter into a treaty which will work well for all of us."

Wolf Chief, very puzzled, seemed deep in thought, but at last he spoke. "You are willing to make a treaty which will supply the wolves with Deer? How could such a treaty benefit the Deer?"

"I see great benefits to my people, oh Wolf Chief," the Chief of the Deer replied. "You, too, will understand in good time. But, first, I would ask that I might dance with your people."

"Of course, oh Chief of the Deer," the Wolf agreed. "We will discuss treaties later."

Wolf Chief then gave orders that the fire should be made bigger. When it was ready the dancers moved into a circle around it. Deer Chief, nimble of foot and quick of movement, danced with the wolves. He was applauded loudly as he made the various movements. All were in great admiration of his dancing.

When the dance had ended Deer Chief rested awhile with Wolf Chief. He carefully avoided any talk about his proposal, a delay which caused Wolf Chief to display some impatience.

"When will we discuss the treaty you propose?" the Wolf finally demanded.

"After I dance for you," the Deer replied. "When my dance is completed you and I will talk. You will soon understand all. Now I wish to dance for your people and for you."

Deer Chief arose and walked slowly toward the fire. He passed close to the Deer slaves who had been allowed to cease their work in order to watch the dancing. As he passed he spoke quietly to them and told them to listen carefully.

"Watch the Hawk who is perched in the tree," he said to them. "When he is ready he will call to you in the manner of Hawks. When the Hawk calls you will all at the same time follow him in the direction he leads. You must do exactly as he commands, without delay or looking back. Do nothing until he calls."

He then moved close to the fire shaking the rawhide thongs he had tied to his legs. He had tied them loose enough so as he walked they hung slightly below his hooves. He shook them toward the fire as he rose on his hind legs and began to prance in a most graceful manner along the edge of the fire. The wolves all watched in awe. They had never seen such a graceful a dancer.

Deer Chief leaped and bucked in the manner of the wild Deer. He circled the fire all the while singing praises in his own language to the fire spirits. The wolves had no idea what he was singing but they liked the sound which was soft and melodious, in stark contrast to the howls which were their songs.

"Oh spirit of the fire warm and bright," Deer Chief sang, "come with me. Warm my people so they might also sing your praises."

He danced several more times around the fire, each time moving the thongs closer to the flames. Suddenly, the fire caught a thong, and the Deer knew his song of praise had been heard by the fire spirits. Once more he circled the fire while singing more praises. A second fire spirit caught another thong and held tightly.

Now Deer Chief began circling ever wider until he had come to the very ring of spectators. In a mighty leap he bounded over the heads of the startled wolves and fled as fast as he could run into the dense forest. Within a few seconds he had disappeared into the protective woods. He could hear the howls of the wolves as they took after him in chase. He also heard the call of the

Hawk and he hoped the Deer slaves would have enough sense to do as they had been bidden.

He ran for quite some time before he could no longer hear the howls of the Wolves and he knew they had given up the chase. Only then did he slow to a more leisurely pace. He looked up and saw the Hawk above. The Hawk's easy flight told him the Deer slaves had made good their escape and were already hidden safely in the forest. They would be able to make their way back to the village in their own time.

Wolf Chief realized he had been tricked by Deer Chief. He appealed to Tyee Sahale that Deer Chief be punished for lying in order to steal fire spirits which belonged to the wolves. Tyee Sahale sent a Raven to the Wolves with his answer.

"Tyee Sahale," the Raven told Wolf Chief, "will not grant your request. Deer Chief did not lie to you. He told you he would talk of treaties when he finished his dance, but the dance remains unfinished. Deer Chief told you his people would benefit and they will. He did not tell you your people would gain anything. He said you would soon understand all and now you do. Deer Chief defeated you fairly. Accept it in good grace."

Then the Raven left.

Wolf Chief then called his people together. He told them they must never again trust anyone who offers a friendly greeting. He told them they must always keep to themselves and listen only to their own counsel. They must avoid contact with anyone who offers treaties and reject all suggestions which appeared to hold advantages gained through mutual cooperation, but offered no guarantees.

That is why, even to this day, the Wolves are rarely seen even though they can be easily heard. It is the reason why they trust no one and cannot be tamed, and why they keep to the forests where they can watch without being seen.

Deer Chief, having arrived safely home, had his people untie the rawhide thongs. The fire spirits still held on tightly and soon they were placed on a pile of dry twigs. The fire spirits began to glow brightly and soon the twigs were burning. The Deer then placed wood logs on the fire and the fire spirits kept the Deer people warm throughout the rest of the winter. The Deer people had the ability to use fire for many years, losing it only when Tyee Sahale took away the animals' magic qualities many centuries later. But that is another story for another time.

Deer Chief was pleased he had managed to outwit Wolf Chief and, of course, he was happy to have returned to his village safely. However, he had not emerged from his adventure totally unscathed. The burning thongs had singed his legs and had caused the white fur to turn black along the sides of his legs near the knees. That is why Deer have black knees to this very day.

Deer Chief had scored a great victory over Wolf Chief, his traditional enemy. He knew the Wolves would be thirsting for vengeance which would place his people in even greater danger than they had known in the past. He called his people together around the fire and related to them the tale of his adventure. He warned them of the dangers they would now face and cautioned them to be wary of strange sounds coming from the underbrush and the thick bushes. He told them to give the Wolves an even wider berth, and to never let up their vigilance while grazing in the meadows. He warned them to be always watchful and to let no one approach in case it might be a Wolf in the disguise of a friendly animal.

That is the reason why to this day a Deer will race away at his fastest speed whenever he hears a twig snap in the forest or when he hears any sound which could be caused by an approaching Wolf.

14 Why the Loon Calls Plaintively
A Lummi Story

Many years ago a small band of the Lummi people lived on the shores of what is now Hood Inlet in the Puget Sound area. Near their village was a large lake. The shamans had forbidden the people to approach it because the lake was the home of an evil spirit. This was held to be true because on several occasions members of the tribe had disappeared without trace while swimming in the lake. It was believed they had all been taken by the evil spirit.

One day a youth told some of the villagers he intended to swim across the lake as a personal achievement. A good swimmer, he had crossed Hood Inlet several times and had completed a swim across the large lake some miles to the west which is now called Lake Quinault. No one doubted his ability to swim the lake, but the village chief, the shaman, and the youth's parents all forbid him to attempt it. The youth, however, was not convinced the lake held an evil spirit. He felt the others had disappeared because they had not been good swimmers and had ventured out too far.

The youth spent many days near the lake looking over the vast expanse of pristine water. He was determined to swim the lake, but he was reluctant to disobey the wishes of his elders. He wondered how he could convince them to allow him to try. As hard as he thought, he could not come up with any idea which would sway them to his way of thinking.

One afternoon temptation got the better of him. He decided to swim the lake without telling anyone. He would prove to the village elders that no spirit, evil or otherwise, lived beneath the cool surface of the lake. He would swim the lake and tell them about it when he returned.

So, without letting anyone know what he was about to do, the youth waded into the lake then began to swim for the far shore. Young and strong, he swam easily with long, powerful strokes. He experienced no difficulty crossing the lake and very soon he waded ashore on the far side. He was no worse for the swim, and he had seen nothing which would indicate the presence of a spirit. He would tell the elders that they had worried for many years for no reason.

As the young warrior sat resting for his return swim he was pleased to see a fat trout swimming idly in shallow water nearby. Using the skills he had learned from watching the bears, he crept up to the fish, and when the moment was right, he swept the fish from the water with a quick scoop of his hand. The trout landed on the beach where the youth killed it by hitting it on the head with a rock.

The boy then made a fire by rubbing two dry sticks together. He cooked the fish and ate it. After his meal he felt tired and could not keep his eyes open. Within a few minutes he was sleeping soundly.

It was nearly sunset when the youth woke to discover he was no longer a tall, muscular young man. He was now a black and white bird. His arms had changed to wings. His legs and feet were now small and set so far back on his body that he could not use them to walk. He knew at once the trout had been sent by the evil lake spirit and had held the magic which changed him into a type of bird he had never before seen.

The youth began to wail in despair. He was lamenting his fate when the evil spirit appeared near the shore in the form of a whirlpool.

"Foolish youth," the whirlpool said. "You violated my sacred lake which is forbidden to humans. In so doing you exposed yourself to my vengeance. You will spend the rest of your time on earth on my lake as the bird which I have caused you to become."

The youth wailed even louder and begged forgiveness, but the lake spirit remained unmoved and would not forgive the foolish young man.

"I will make two concessions to you and two only. I will give you a voice which will produce beautiful, but sad, calls. You may use those calls to warn away other foolish mortals who will come to visit my lake. The second concession will be to bring you a mate. I have decided to ensure an endless family of my fine new birds. I am pleased with the appearance you have and I will consider you to be my child."

The stricken youth, realizing he was doomed to remain forever as a strange bird never before seen on earth, wailed until the whirlpool disappeared beneath the surface. Then, knowing he was wasting his time, he sat back to consider his next move. At length he decided he might escape if he could fly. He waddled as best he could into the lake.

Once in the lake he found he could swim with a wondrous graceful motion. He could dive and swim under the surface for great distances. He decided to see if he could fly. He swam to the edge of the lake, turned and began to flap his wings and paddle as fast as he could with his stubby feet. Although he needed a fair amount of water to lift off, he was elated to find he could fly.

He had escaped the clutches of the evil spirit. Joyfully, he flew to his village and called out to his mother. To her, however, the bird's plaintive call meant nothing and, having never before seen such a creature, she feared it. She beat at it with her broom whenever it came near. Her husband, hearing her screams, came running out of the lodge. Seeing the strange bird swoop down on his wife and fearing it was attacking her, he threw stones at it to drive it away.

The youth, sorrowful once more, realized he would have to accept the cost of his disobedience. He also knew that he would have to return to the spirit's lake and remain there forever.

When he landed once again on the lake he recalled the spirit's words about using his calls to warn others from venturing into the forbidden lake. This he did from that day forward.

The evil spirit, true to his word, eventually gave to the youth a mate, a maiden who had not heeded the warnings and had also swam in the lake. She, too, became one of the strange birds. The two accepted their fate and grew to care deeply for each other.

In time they built a nest and produced other birds. When the family grew large, the lake spirit gave some of them permission to leave and find other lakes. That is why there are loons on nearly every lake along the coast. The Indians have named them in many different ways. However, by whatever name these unusual birds are given, a literal translation is often *Giver of Warnings*.

The tribes of the Puget Sound area told the story of the first loon as a warning to their children whenever young ones dared to disobey their elders.

15 Why Women have Cold Feet
A Tsimshian Story

That women throughout the ages have been afflicted with cold feet is well documented. Reference to this phenomena is found in various chronicles and literary works ranging from the Dark Ages to modern times. Whether this unusual characteristic is a deficiency in the female circulatory system or has some other reason is best left to discussion within scientific circles. Some ancient societies considered the cause as being everything from God's punishment on Eve for wading in a forbidden stream to a curse inflicted on women by a Saxon witch just before she perished in her ordeal by water for crimes she claimed were false.

The Pacific Coast Indians have their own versions. As might be expected every version differed in varying degrees, but the majority are similar to the story told by the Tsimshian people. Perhaps because the Tsimshian lived so far north and therefore had more than a passing acquaintance with North Wind explains why they seem to know so much about cold feet. It is reasonable to expect they would be more knowledgeable than the Cowichan or Capilano who lived further south and enjoyed longer summers and milder winters. It seems fitting, therefore, that we accept the Tsimshian story simply because they would seem to be more suited as the authorities on the subject.

In the very early days, even before the arrival of the Tsimshian People, the world was the domain of four great wind chiefs. These were the most powerful of all the winds.

The greatest of all was North Wind who, because he was so strong, had taken half of the year all for himself. He had decreed the months of October to April as being his, and the other three

145

could divide the remaining months among themselves. Because of North Wind's greed, half the year was always very cold indeed.

However, Ka'ah, the great Raven God, limited North Wind to the territory of the north lands, and ordered him never to venture into the southern half of the world. He also ordered North Wind to sleep during the months of May to September. The three other chiefs were content with the arrangement and got along well enough in their smaller kingdoms.

South Wind, gentle by nature unless angered, kept the forests green and the grass thick and plentiful. South Wind had four sons, three of whom were very strong. His eldest son was Big Rain, his second son was Gray Cloud, and his third son was Water Higher than a Man's Knees. This son had an extremely violent temper and would cause floods if provoked. Fortunately, he was not angered often. The fourth son, the smallest, was a quiet spirit called Hopper of Hedges. He traveled as a gentle zephyr and rustled the grass as he passed by. The flowers would nod their pretty heads to him as he went about his business. Everyone loved the fourth son.

South Wind's pride and joy, however, was his fifth child, his beautiful daughter whom he had named Early Morning Breeze. Of all his family she was the most beloved. Her four brothers were devoted to her and she was devoted to them.

East Wind had two sons. The oldest was called Evening Breeze. The youngest was named Red Face. Red Face would venture out on occasion to look out over the world. He could be seen either in the western sky or the eastern sky and was a messenger of the weather spirit. If he looked out from the west the next day would bring fine weather, but if he looked out from the east the day would bring rain and cold. After humans arrived on the earth they soon learned to watch for Red Face, especially the fishermen and hunters. They would then know what kind of weather to expect and would plan their trips accordingly.

West Wind had two sons also. Both were responsible for bringing the warm weather from the ocean and worked together. The eldest was called Sea Breeze. The younger son was named Pink Cloud. They were both gentle spirits.

North Wind was father to twins, a boy named Snow and a girl named Ice. When Snow was of age he went to his father and asked that a suitable bride be found for him and a marriage arranged. North Wind decided the ideal wife for his son would be Early Morning Breeze. North Wind sent Snow's cousin, Freezing Rain, to the kingdom of South Wind as an emissary to make the arrangements.

South Wind was reluctant to make the match, but he was afraid of the power of North Wind so he agreed to it.

Early Morning Breeze was not at all happy. She had hoped to marry gentle Evening Breeze, the son of East Wind. She was, however, a dutiful daughter and would obey her father. She prepared for her journey to the kingdom of North Wind, but on the morning of her departure she wept. Her tears fell to the grass and Ka'ah, seeing her distress, ordered that tears would appear on the grass for all time from that day forward. To this day we see drops of dew on the grass every morning during the warm weather months and these are in honor of the gentle spirit, Early Morning Breeze.

Early Morning Breeze married Snow whereupon North Wind held a great potlatch which lasted many days. Then, all the guests departed leaving the unhappy girl with her husband.

Early Morning Breeze and Snow were not at all compatible. Neither shared the other's interests and the land of North Wind was far too cold for the girl. She was confined to the lodge because she dared not venture out into the cold which was too intense for her. She became more and more unhappy and, had it not been for the true friendship of her sister-in-law, Ice, she would have perished from loneliness.

Eventually, North Wind realized the marriage he had arranged would never succeed. Snow complained that his bride would not accompany him on his travels because of her aversion to the cold. He could not understand why she did not like cold weather so Snow grew very miserable. Although he was not a bad spirit, he soon grew impatient with his bride and threatened to harm her. Early Morning Breeze grew fearful for her life.

North Wind, who had chosen Early Morning Breeze only because he had envisioned her bringing some cheer to his bleak kingdom, was furious. He vented his rage upon the world by causing everything to freeze. Throughout his half of the world all the land was covered in snow and ice. He kept it thus for many years. He would not allow the warm weather spirit to enter his lands.

The time came when Early Morning Breeze could no longer continue with the life she had been forced into. The unhappy woman decided to seek help from her family. She carved a duck from a piece of wood, breathed life into it, and told it to fly south to the kingdom of South Wind with a message.

The duck did as it was commanded and hurried south. There he found South Wind, East Wind, and West Wind waging a fierce battle against the forces of North Wind. All the efforts of the three great chiefs were just enough to hold off the forces of North Wind, Snow, and all their relatives.

"Oh, mighty South Wind," the duck said. "Your beautiful daughter no longer smiles, and her cold husband plans to banish her from the lodge upon his return from the wars. She sent me to tell you this."

South Wind was enraged. He called his four sons to him and told them of the duck's message. He knew all their forces combined were not enough to defeat North Wind. Indeed, they had been fortunate to prevent his advancement into the southern half of the world. A plan was desperately needed, he told them.

The oldest son, Big Rain, volunteered to rescue his sister. He gathered all his magic and, disguised as a gigantic black cloud, drifted north. North Wind, however, saw through his ploy and turned the cloud into a fierce hail storm. Big Rain fell to the ground as a huge mound of ice where he remained, unable to move.

Gray Cloud, the second son, then tried. He was also seen and North Wind turned him into sleet. He also fell to the ground.

The third son then tried. But he, too, was seen as he tried to sneak in from the east. North Wind turned him into a giant glacier. He remained on the ground unable to move except for an inch at a time. He knew it would take thousands of years to reach his sister.

The fourth son, Hopper of Hedges, decided to try an idea. He moved slowly north traveling at night disguised as a long wispy cloud. He spent the days absolutely still, lying close to the ground. North Wind saw him but did not see that he was his enemy. The cloud moved very slowly through the valleys. It followed the rivers until it entered the kingdom of North Wind. He continued as he had planned, and though he was seen by many of North Wind's family, none thought he was an enemy.

Eventually he found his brothers. He thawed them back to their proper shapes and they continued on their way. The older brothers agreed to obey Hopper of Hedges because his plan was seen to be working. They hid beneath the long cloud and remained unseen. In that way the four sons of South Wind made their way into the middle of North Wind's kingdom.

The four brothers then called on all their magic powers. They poured rain onto the land and caused hot breezes to blow. Soon all the north was flooded. North Wind hurried back to do battle but he was too late. As North Wind retreated the three great chiefs followed and soon there was so much water North Wind could not prevail against it. Finally, North Wind was forced to appeal to the brothers for terms of peace.

"Leave me alone," he cried out in anguish. "Take your sister and go."

The brothers now realized that North Wind had been truly defeated and was at their mercy. They talked with him and forced upon him harsh terms. He was made to agree that six months of the year was too much for one wind, and he was forced to give up three of his months. One month was given to each of the other chiefs so that each wind had a season equal to all others.

North Wind howled with rage when he was told the terms he was expected to accept. The brothers simply told him he would either accept or they would renew their assault on his lands for a full year. He then agreed to keep within the three months of December, January and February for all time. Sometimes he breaks his promise, but generally he keeps his word.

Having settled that problem, the five children of South Wind prepared for their return home. They were just about to fly away when a plaintive voice was heard calling out.

"Please take me with you. I wish to live also in the south."

It was Ice who was calling. The five agreed to take her with them because she had been kind to Early Morning Breeze over the years. North Wind objected. He wailed in despair at the though of losing his only daughter. There were further talks and it was agreed finally that Ice could go to the south and live on a high mountain during the summer months. She would return to her father's kingdom for the winter. All were agreeable to the arrangement and the six prepared to leave.

Early Morning Breeze told her friend to hold tightly to her feet. She carried her friend in that manner all the way to South Wind's kingdom. There she was placed safely atop the mountain now called Mount Baker. That is why the top of Mount Baker is white all summer.

In her haste to leave the lodge of her despised husband, Early Morning Breeze had neglected to put on her moccasins. Ice, of course, had frigid hands and the cold caused Early Morning Breeze's feet to become so cold they were never warm again. In memory of this, South Wind passed his daughter's cold feet on to all women when Great Spirit put humans on his world. This is why women have cold feet.

16 Why Crows Hop When They Walk

A Kwakiutl Story

In flight a crow is a graceful bird. He soars on outstretched wings, seemingly able to glide on air currents with no effort whatsoever. On the ground he is not at all graceful. He does not walk in the manner of other birds that hop along with even steps. The crow hops unevenly or takes short jumps. He never seems to have both feet on the ground at the same time unless he is standing still. His unusual walk came about hundreds of years ago after the first Crow lost a contest and proved to be a poor loser.

During the early days of the world, when only birds and animals lived here, Crow was an able hunter and a hard worker. He kept his family well fed and owned a fine lodge for them to live in. Crow was proud of his achievements and began to boast about what he had and the things he had accomplished. It was not long before the others who lived in the village began to tire of his continual bragging. One day, the other birds and animals decided something had to be done to stop Crow from being so boastful. They called a meeting to discuss the problem.

Choosing a day when they knew Crow would be away on a fishing trip, the villagers gathered to talk. Everyone was there—Beaver, Raccoon, Wolf, Cougar, Raven. Owl, Mouse, and Skunk also attended. All agreed that Crow would have to be taught a lesson which would stop his bragging. Many ideas were put forward but none were workable.

At length, Kwi'kwa, the Eagle asked to speak. Kwi'kwa was considered very wise by the others so they all listened intently to his words.

151

"I have noticed," said Kwi'kwa, "that Crow is indeed a mighty hunter. I have also noticed that he uses snares and traps. He never uses a bow and arrow while he hunts. Why would this be?"

"It is," interjected Kl'ay, the Bear, "because Crow is not at all good with a bow. He is excellent with a spear, but he does poorly with the bow."

"Exactly," replied the Eagle. "We must use that weakness to our advantage."

After a few minutes of thought, Bu'di, the Cougar spoke. "I have an idea," he said. "Let us arrange an archery contest. The rules will apply as they always do, but we will add an extra one. The loser will be required to dance before the others while they shoot arrows at his feet. Because Crow will surely lose, his humiliation should be enough to curb his boasting for all time. Crow is not likely to forget such a disgrace."

The others agreed the idea was a good one, but some doubted that Crow would enter such a contest. They reasoned he would not be able to win and, therefore, would stay out of it.

"He will enter," prophesied Bu'di. "He will enter because he has grown so vain that he will never admit to being a poor archer. If he does not enter the contest, he will admit this and his vanity will not permit such an admission."

The villagers then drew up the plans for the archery contest and, pleased with their conspiracy, awaited the big day when Crow would meet his comeuppance.

On the day of the contest all the hunters assembled in a clearing. Targets were erected in their places and all was made ready. Crow, as Cougar had predicted, appeared and entered his name among the lists of archers. The contest began and, as expected, Crow did very poorly indeed coming in dead last with a very low score.

Because he had lost the contest, he agreed he must abide by the rules and accept the ordeal of dancing before the others while they shot arrows at his feet. In their jubilation over what they felt was their great victory, they all failed to see the sparkle in Crow's eyes. Had they seen it they might have worried because they would have known Crow was up to something.

The drumming began. The hunters lined up with their bows and a good supply of arrows as Crow walked to the center of the clearing. He began to dance. He danced so nimbly and so well that he easily dodged the arrows which were missing his feet by mere inches. Suddenly, to the dismay of all the archers, it occurred to them that Crow was enjoying himself. He had turned the tables on them. Their arrows and stamina and patience wore out long before Crow showed any sign whatever of growing tired.

"I have lost the archery contest," Crow sang out merrily as he danced, "but I am winning this contest."

He danced around easily avoiding the arrows which fell around him. His taunting song continued for as long as the others shot their arrows.

Finally, the archers called a halt. They had to admit that Crow had not been humiliated. Indeed, he had made them look quite foolish. One by one they drifted away with Crow's laughter ringing in their ears.

No one knew it at the time, but the contest had also been watched by Q'an'iquel'ukwha, the great god who made changes in the world whenever he deemed changes to be necessary. Q'an'iquel'ukwha had watched Crow turn humiliation into victory and had been pleased—until Crow began to taunt the others. This type of boasting was not pleasing to the mighty god. He made a magic sign over Crow even as he hopped about in his dance. Crow had been so elated by his victory over his tormentors that he had not even noticed they had all left. He was singing and dancing for himself, laughing at them.

Crow, alone in the clearing, finally stopped dancing. He took a few minutes to rest then arose and turned to walk back to his lodge. But he could not walk in his usual way. He found he could only manage an ungainly hop. Alarmed, he sat against a large rock for some time. He thought he was only tired from his long exertion. However, when he again tried to walk, he found he could still only hop in awkward little steps.

Q'an'iquel'ukwha had punished Crow by transforming him from a graceful walker into the awkward hopper he is to this very day. That is the reason why crows, so graceful in flight, are awkward while on the ground.

Epilogue

The natives of the Pacific Coast had developed what was possibly the highest culture of all North American indigenous people. Its complex simplicity was a major factor in its success. From an economic and social point of view, the entire structure was unique.

Except during periods when wars were waged, the various bands engaged in trade and other forms of social endeavor. Fishermen traded their harvest for furs and meat with hunters. Carpenters and artisans traded their work and skills for payment. This trading extended outside individual villages to other tribes up and down the coast.

The Chinook tribes traded goods among the coastal tribes as well as those living in the interior. These traders moved throughout a wide area as far east as the Rocky Mountains, south to northern California, and they were known to the tribes who lived in the northern part of British Columbia.

The Chinooks were to the West Coast what the Neutrals were to Ontario and the Ohio Valley. Like the Neutrals, the Chinooks moved freely within other territories buying, selling, and bartering. They accepted anything of value in payment—silver, copper, furs, food, and the highly prized he-ah-qua, the coastal equivalent of wampum, which was considered very valuable. Like wampum it was made of shells and had a value which varied according to the length of the string.

The Chinooks were a collection of many tribes and their zeal as traders did much to bring about an understanding of what each nation meant to the others. Just as they brought the art of trading to various tribes, they also brought about much of what caused the decline of the coastal society. The Chinooks unwittingly extended the custom of potsha'tl.

Potsha'tl, which literally means *giving*, had humble beginnings far back in Nootka history. The event was originally a simple ritual held under traditional rules. The occasion had to be joyous and the host bestowed his guests with gifts, the value of which denoted the status and importance of the guest. A chief or a shaman would likely be given a fine fur, while a fisherman might be given a fishing spear of excellent workmanship. In its humble beginnings potsha'tl was the Nootka version of our marriage or christening ceremonies, the only difference being the recipients of the gifts.

For a wedding potsha'tl there was one great difference from the others—the only gift given by the host was the bride's dowry. This single gift was usually all the woman's family could afford. Because the dowry included the family totem figures and heritage myths, a young warrior could obtain instant glory and honor by marrying the daughter of a legendary warrior. All he had to do was accept the dowry, and he always did because to refuse it would have been a gross insult to the bride's family. Such an insult would probably have caused an all out war. The merging of families meant a merger of honors, an alliance of strength, and often an increase in fortunes for both sides.

As the years went by the potsha'tl evolved until it lost its original intent. Tribal chiefs began to use the potsha'tl as a vehicle to spread the word of their power and prestige. Newly ascended chiefs would host great parties to celebrate their high status, to flaunt their wealth, and to impress their guests. This was usually done through extravagant gift giving. By enhancing his esteem in the eyes of his neighbors, a new chief could put his less wealthy rivals down a notch or two and make it less likely for his village to be seen as an easy prize to be seized through war.

The potsha'tl did not always work out as the chief intended. Sometimes his show of wealth brought on jealousies which caused others to cast covetous eyes on his possessions. Such situations could easily end in war.

Eventually, as might be imagined, the potsha'tl became an unmanageable monster. As it spread further afield it was adapted and modified until it became, to a great degree, ritualistic. Eventually the Chinooks introduced the custom to the inland tribes, by this time the ceremony had become the potlatch.

Each tribe had its own reasons and motives for holding a potlatch. But whatever the reason, the main purpose was always to impress others. The outlay of goods was always excessive and wasteful. Great quantities of food were consumed by the guests, and on the final day overly generous amounts of food were pressed upon the departing revellers for their journey home. Gifts of robes made of animal skins or hair were thrust upon the guests. Ornaments made of copper (the Indians valued copper over gold) were given away. Long strings of he-ah-qua were distributed with abandon. The more wealth a tribe gave away, the higher it was held in esteem—or so it was thought.

At the end of the festivities, which could last several days, the guests, laden with food and gifts, would stagger away on their voyage home. The guests might not know it, but often they left their hosts totally bankrupt of material wealth. Many were the villages whose inhabitants were doomed to face a long, bleak winter without enough blankets to keep warm or enough food to ensure proper nourishment. No matter—their esteem among their peers was assured. Their show of wealth and power would have convinced any potential enemy of the futility of attacking a people of such power. Besides, such generosity could not be repaid with treachery. Generosity alone would suffice.

This was the true disadvantage of the potlatch. In the long run it did not pay to be invited to a potlatch, for attendance imposed an obligation. The members of a village which had, through its chief, accepted an invitation to a potlatch were expected to repay the honor within a reasonable time by hosting a potlatch grander than the one they had just left. In other words, one good potlatch deserved another, and the value of the gifts to be given were expected to be at least equal to the value of those received. It was eventually expected that the gifts exceed the value of those given as a matter of honor.

Therefore, immediately upon returning to his own lands, a chief would begin planning his own potlatch. In the meantime, should he be invited to a second one within the same year, he was obliged to attend. The gifts received at the second celebration were simply added to the list of obligations.

Potlatch was held throughout the year, but mainly during the summer. There were winter potlatch celebrations, but these were dedicated to the koo'syoot, the various secret societies which all tribes had. The Kwakiutl alone had twenty-eight secret societies. During the koo'syoot ceremonies, novices were initiated and became part of the koo'syoot with all the rights and privileges of membership. These ceremonies included dramatizations of rituals inherent in the rites of the secret societies. During these dramas the members danced, sang, and recited stories which praised their ancestors—both real and mystic. The idea was to advertise the ancestral exploits of both the tribe and the individual families. The dancers, wearing brightly colored carved masks and ceremonial robes, were transformed figuratively into the mythical creatures they were praising.

However, it was the potlatch that was the focal point of the culture, and in their efforts to outdo each other, entire villages, bands, and individual families suffered complete bankruptcy. It was not long before less wealthy chiefs lost everything they owned and their relatives' wealth as well.

Then, as if the situation had not deteriorated enough, some of the very powerful chiefs, having grown bored with mundane celebrations, invented a new, grimmer type of potlatch. The new game proved to be the final scrum in the deadly contest of one-upmanship. The change belatedly forced both the Canadian and the United States governments to introduce firm measures.

The new potlatch was a totally perverse, evil reversal of the original potsha'tl. In this version nothing was given away. Instead, possessions were destroyed outright. In elaborate ceremonies, furs, lodges, skins, and artifacts of the most beautiful jade and argillite were burned or otherwise destroyed. Huge, beautifully decorated war canoes were dragged into the ocean and sunk or set aflame. In some ceremonies the village slaves were killed, while in others they were set free and lost as possessions. All this was done to impress upon others that a particular village or chief was so wealthy, so powerful, that even wanton destruction of property could not diminish his powerful medicine.

157

Federal authorities, at the insistence of provincial and state governments, stepped in and banned the potlatch. The Canadian government had always viewed the potlatch with disapproval, but had allowed the practice to continue. The governments of British Columbia, Oregon, and Washington had also turned a blind eye to the situation, despite the warnings of missionaries, social educators, and groups of concerned natives. When reports of wholesale destruction began coming in, all levels of government were forced to act—and they acted with a belated vengeance.

The various authorities wielded a collective heavy hand. In 1884 all potlatch ceremonies were prohibited. The rule applied to all, even to small harmless ceremonies that were confined to one or two villages. The prohibition cut a wide swath. Only the Haida, who lived so far to the north that they were difficult to police, continued the potlatch awhile longer.

The potlatch, in its earlier form, had been the key to the cultural and social pattern of the coastal tribes. Once control was lost and the decrees ended the practice, the disintegration of the Pacific tribal society entered its final phase.

Without the potlatch there was little reason for individual tribes to continue social ties with their neighbors. Commercial ties, already weakened by the arrival of the white traders, finally unraveled when Chinook traders ceased their travels, quietly capitulating to the men of the Hudson's Bay Company, the Northwest Company, and other white trading interests. Without social and commercial interests there was no reason to fraternize.

The various bands remained largely isolated, each in its own area. The children were whisked away in a disgraceful and inhumane manner to mission schools where, while being taught the ways of the white world, they were denied the ways of their own.

Within a few years the social environment of Canada's Pacific natives declined to thirty-one poorly managed reserves scattered along the mainland and Vancouver Island. They no longer represented a viable society—they were a scattered people with no voice. The natives of Washington and Oregon fared little better.

The Thunderbird retreated to his cave in the highest mountain. Tyee Sahale no longer visited his people through the words of the shamans. Tsin, Fair Weather Woman, and Master Carpenter moved deeper into the lands of mists. Itopolos, the Coyote God, stopped his work, and Raven Who Walks the Land was seen no more in Haida-Gwai. The gods of the people retreated to their homes in the sky and there they remained. The signs they left are the only proof of their ever being on earth.

These signs are present in everyday life. Blue Jay remains a mischievous, raucous bird unable to sing, acting without thought as he plays his tricks on unwary campers. Crow still lords it over Raven. Deer's knees are black. Raccoon's eyes are masked. Owl still eats Skunk when he catches him. The four chief winds blow within their assigned seasons. The tides continue to ebb and flow in accordance with the treaty agreed to by Wolf Chief and Raccoon Chief so long ago. Beaver will still go out of his way to avoid a meeting with Porcupine. Loon calls plaintively to warn children of the danger within his lakes.

The supernatural Bears remain the quarry of the five Wolves in the darkness of the night sky. The supernatural Salmon is pursued to this day by the two fishermen. On a clear night when the moon is full, if you look up you can easily see Kwa'te and his wife, the Frog Princess, walking across the surface.

Thunderbird, however, has not forgotten his children. He often ventures forth, when the clouds are thick, to fly across his lands. His great wings make a fearsome noise as he proceeds on his journey. There is a message in the sound.

Thunderbird is telling his people that they must never forget their past. He is telling them to rekindle the fires of interest, to remember the ancient tales so they might be retold, teaching the children of what once was.

His message, it appears, is being heard. The totem carvers have once again taken up their tools. The sculptors of jade have resumed their art. Painters are once again committing the likeness of birds and animals to board and canvas, and the pictures show the birds and animals as they were so long ago, fully garbed in the bright robes they once wore. Dancers and singers have relearned their music. The culture, once thought lost, is returning.

The fire from Thunderbird's eyes has rekindled the flame of interest among the native people of the Pacific Coast. Hopefully it will never be lost again.

Bibliography

Clutesi, G. *Potlatch*. Sidney, B.C.: Gray's Publishing, 1969. Recommended reading.

Curtis, Edward S. *The North American Indian*. Volume 10. Cambridge, Massachusetts: University Press, 1915.

Goldman, I. *The Kwakiutl on Vancouver Island*. New York: McGraw-Hill, 1937.

Halliday, W. M. *Potlatch and Totem*. Toronto: Dent & Company, 1935.

LaViolette, F. E. *The Struggle For Survival: Indian Cultures and the Protestant Ethic in British Columbia*. University of Toronto, 1961.

Leachman, Douglas. *Native Tribes of Canada*. Toronto: W. J. Gage, 1957. Recommended reading.

McFeat, Tom. *Indians of the North Pacific Coast*. Toronto: McClelland and Stewart, 1966. Recommended reading.

Woodcock, George. *Peoples of the Coast: Indians of the Pacific Northwest*. Edmonton: Hurtig Publishers, 1977.